The Saints

The Saints

A Short History

SIMON YARROW

OXFORD
UNIVERSITY PRESS

OXFORD

UNIVERSITY PRESS

Great Clarendon Street, Oxford, OX2 6DP,
United Kingdom

Oxford University Press is a department of the University of Oxford.
It furthers the University's objective of excellence in research, scholarship,
and education by publishing worldwide. Oxford is a registered trade mark of
Oxford University Press in the UK and in certain other countries

Published in the United States of America by Oxford University Press
198 Madison Avenue, New York, NY 10016, United States of America

British Library Cataloguing in Publication Data
Data available

Library of Congress Control Number: 2016933494

ISBN 978-0-19-878438-8

Printed in Great Britain by
Clays Ltd, St Ives plc

CONTENTS

ACKNOWLEDGEMENTS

Writing a book about saints, especially a brief one, can be an intimidating experience. Everyone is familiar with what kind of thing a saint is. We all know about heroes; people who embody qualities we would wish for ourselves, and who might champion our causes. But saints are a type of hero quite distinct from Greek or Roman, Hindu or Buddhist heroes. And their modern surrogates, film and pop stars, sporting greats, and superheroes, resemble them only superficially. The task of separating saints from the heroic crowd is followed by one of differentiation among sainthood's myriad manifestations in historically particular Christian communities and confessions. A vast and diverse topic, the history of saints can lead one outwards into deep philosophical and spiritual waters, and inwards to the contemplation of our most intimate and disturbing desires, fears, and hopes. In writing this book I have tried to follow as many diverse pathways as possible whilst keeping an eye on the highway. This is not an exhaustive list of saints, or a series of biographies piled one atop the other, and I am sorry if your favourite saint is not included here. There are plenty of good dictionaries for those who are looking for a reference work on saints. I have tried instead to offer a selection of portraits in landscapes, to show how sainthood was historically constructed, contested, and embodied out of the divine calls to holiness visited upon individuals, and through collective responses to the political and social pressures that prevailed upon communities.

I was thrilled to be invited by Andrea Keegan to contribute to such a celebrated series of books. Chloe Musson and Carrie Hickman have been immensely supportive in recent weeks, and the prompt copy-editing of Michael Janes and proofreading by Gillian Northcott Liles was hugely appreciated. But my largest debt of gratitude within OUP is owed to Jenny Nugee, a consummate professional with tremendous patience and good cheer. A book such as this depends a great deal on the scholarship of others. If I can only encourage interested readers to pick up some of the fine works indicated in the further reading sections then I would consider my efforts a success.

My time as Visiting Research Fellow at the University of Connecticut Humanities Institute (2011–13) was partly taken up with preparing the book in its early stages. I have fond memories of the collegial atmosphere there, and I am particularly thankful to the UCHI for the conversations it enabled me to have, and for the friendships I was able to establish with, to name a few among many, Brendan Kane, Gregory Semenza, Christopher Clark, Bob Hasenfratz, Dan Caner, Lindy Brady, and Sharon Harris. I am grateful also to the anonymous readers of OUP for helping me to see how I might develop my ideas, and to my own informally appointed readers, John Arnold, Simon Ditchfield, Chris Callow, Bob Moore, William Purkis, and Diarmaid MacCulloch, who saved me from error and from occasional despair. I would like to thank Chris O'Malley for helping me with even greater despairs, Nicholas White for his painstaking efforts in reading the manuscript, Marina Frid in helping me secure use of an image, and Christopher Evans for his generosity in the role of intelligent lay reader. I thank Nancy Evans for the joy she brings to my life, and for the budding little hero she has brought into the world in the shape of Arthur our son. Finally, because of her constantly supportive, nurturing presence throughout my life, I dedicate this book to Kath Weightman, homemaker, teacher, epicurean hostess, and storyteller.

LIST OF ILLUSTRATIONS

List of Illustrations

1

Introduction

Superheroes, Heroes, and Saints

Let's begin with Kal-El, better known as Superman. Everyone knows his story. Superman comes from a dying planet, cast into the universe by his father in an inter-stellar seedpod. He fetches up in the American Midwest, human in form but with superhuman power, an orphan-alien adopted by an elderly, childless couple. His childhood is an education in self-restraint and kindness; his values appear homespun and gauche to metropolitan citizens, although they turn out to be an exemplar of a civic good with which they have lost touch.

Superman was the invention of Jerry Siegel and Joe Schuster, the sons of Eastern European Jewish immigrants to early twentieth-century Cleveland, Ohio. Superman's story is a fantasy of Jewish assimilation to modern America: Kal-El is Moses cast among the bulrushes by his father, Jor-El (both are Hebrew-sounding prophets' names, think of Joel, Daniel, Ezekiel). Superman is as strong as Samson and a model of American gentile masculinity; the all-American *goy* counterpart to his innocently bewildered, *nebbish* alter

Figure 1 'Is it a bird? Is it a plane? No, it's St Nicholas!' Bicci di Lorenzo (Italian, 1373-1452) *St Nicholas of Bari Banishing the Storm* (Ashmolean Museum).

ego, Clark Kent. The Christian cult of saints arose out of the same classical Greek and Hebrew heritage as that of Superman. In fact, the family resemblance (see Figure 1) was emphasized in *Superman Returns* (2006), in a series of rather unsubtle associations made for evangelical Christian movie-goers between Superman and the archetype of every saint—Jesus Christ. 'Another nice Jewish boy resurrected as a Christian god', was the acute and gently mischievous observation of the film by the philosopher and comic book buff, Harry Brod.

The Logic of Sainthood

Heroes are universal to human culture. Their appeal lies in a natural desire for us to admire others, to look up to them as models to imitate and to think of them as our friends and patron-protectors (the original Greek meaning of the word). As we shall see, saints, the inheritors of classical heroic antecedents, are very special kinds of heroes, the results of two-thousand-year-old living Christian traditions, yet distinct from those early heroes of antiquity, for the path they follow towards God is through Jesus Christ.

The lives of the saints are still a living reality in the consciousness of different Christian traditions today. On 27 April 2014 the Catholic Church came together to witness the canonization of Popes John Paul II and John XXIII. Leading the canonization mass, Pope Francis I proclaimed: 'We declare and define Blessed John XXIII and John Paul II to be saints and we enrol them among the saints, decreeing that they are to be venerated as such by the whole church.' In this canonization ceremony, performed before an audience of 800,000 pilgrims in Rome, and televised worldwide to millions, the Church acknowledged both men as having shown sufficient virtue in their lives to have merited the immediate company of God. For Roman Catholics this was a joyous occasion that refreshed faiths and opened up new associations between the faithful and heaven, strengthening the work of the Church in the world. Any study of the saints must acknowledge the historical richness of their appeal within the institutional church and beyond it among diffuse communities of the faithful.

Many popular directories of saints exist today that give brief details of their lives, and their powers to intervene in one specialist cause or another. North Americans of no faith and of faiths other than Christianity know to bury a statue of St Joseph in their yards for a quick sale of their property.

The English look to the ninth-century bishop of Winchester, St Swithun, on the 15 July for signs of the summer to come. If it rains on that day then it will continue to rain for forty more days. The love-struck and lonely hearted of the world are free to declare their crushes with a card or flowers to the object of their affections, signing in the name of a proxy, St Valentine, on the 14 February. Such is the domination of TV schedules by the Gothic horror genre, the 'vamdram', that contemporary popular culture might do well to remember St Marcellus of Paris, the fifth-century bishop known in some versions of his life as a slayer of vampires. St Augustine would be delighted to know that he was recently elected the patron saint of bloggers, whilst St Christina the Astonishing, the thirteenth-century Belgian nun famed for her rather eccentric behaviour might well have mixed feelings for her patronal association with psychiatrists. (Nick Cave's album 'Henry's Dream' has a song all about her.)

A saint is a person who by various means has demonstrated such worth during their lifetime as to posthumously merit the company of God. The saint (Latin *sanctus, sancta,* male, female) is a 'holy one', someone whose exemplary and exceptional qualities bring them close to God. But how is saintly merit defined and acquired? How can one be sure of a saint's closeness to God and posthumous presence in heaven? Do saints need official endorsement or special witnesses or followers to confirm their status? Or is saintliness an intensely private and mysterious relationship that need concern none but an individual and their god? This book will help us to answer these questions.

Where Does Sanctity Come From?

There is an unavoidable paradox in the study of saints, which has implications for the way this book has been written. Thomas Carlyle published *On Heroes and Hero Worship* in 1841 as a series of lectures expounding the Great Man theory of history. Despite hardly mentioning saints in this work Carlyle owed much to the theology of his Calvinist childhood in his universal definition of the hero. His heroes were not products of their environment nor were they solely priests or prophets but included pagan deities, men of letters, poets, and kings. They were divinely struck flints that set light to their times, 'the great man, with his free force, direct out of God's own hand, is the lightening'. Carlyle's heroes make for an odd assortment of imaginary dinner guests; including the Norse god Odin, the Muslim prophet Muhammad, the Florentine poet of the *Inferno*, Dante, and the diminutive dictator, Napoleon, as well as the more predictable Protestant heroes Martin Luther and John Knox. In a nod to the humanity at the heart of Christian worship, Carlyle approvingly identified hero-worship as 'the germ of Christianity itself'.

The anthropologists Jean and John Comaroff offer a startlingly different view of heroes and heroism. They see heroism as the product of complex processes of social creativity. The German sociologist Max Weber called this 'attributive charisma', the result of acts of nomination and advocacy reflecting collective aspiration, the spark of sanctity identified here with the wishes of the people. But like Carlyle, Weber also insisted on charisma as being the 'gift', 'germ', or 'kernel' within heroic individuals, an essence that bludgeoned and beguiled the faithful with a graceful assault on their imaginations. (This reflects the filtering of the word 'charisma' into Christianity through Greek translations of the Hebrew Bible, carrying with it a sense of conferred, transfiguring grace.) For Carlyle heroes and great men follow the saints in being supreme examples of creatures who honour their Creator. For the Comaroffs the saint is almost a cipher for social aspirations, desires, and creativity; saints being informally elected or invented to suit worldly needs.

It seems then that we encounter saints in that space where, as Stanley Tambiah succinctly observes, 'what goes up must come down'. In tracing sanctity's historical trajectories we need to remember that saints belong beside God in Heaven, *and* down among the people of their *cultus* (the Latin collective noun for their devotees). It follows that wherever the lives of the faithful are thought to converge with the presence of God, that is where we might find sanctity, whether that be in the body of living saints, or preserved in miraculous signs, or detected in the places they once visited. The Roman Catholic Church attempted to manage this holy collision of saint and cult in the late twelfth and thirteenth centuries with the reservation of canonization to the papacy, and went on to consolidate it in the Tridentine Reforms of the sixteenth and seventeenth centuries, and in further reforms of the twentieth century. What this tells us is that canonization has often been just as much a political, sociological, and diplomatic matter as a religious concern. Wherever we encounter saints, we shall need to ask by means of whom or what is veneration directed towards the saint?

The cult of St Francis of Assisi was assured when in 1228 the papacy canonized him within two years of his death and without official enquiry. This did not prevent disputes between rival interpreters of Francis's legacy and its position on apostolic poverty. In his simultaneous canonization of St John Paul II and St John XXIII, the current Pope (St Francis's modern namesake) offered a salve to divergent tendencies within the Catholic Church today. All three examples illustrate the tendency summed up in Stanley Tambiah's gravitational theory of holiness: humans become saints by turning from the world for higher causes, but their holy power resounds only on the terms by which the world comprehends it.

In this way we might think of saints as both map and compass, denoted by a 'magnetic north' that points towards the divine, and a 'true north', allocated to them by human beings. Saints never entirely escape the world. But their relics, clothes, and personal effects, and the places they visited, offer the rest of us a path to the divine.

We shall have cause to keep these two points of navigational reference in mind throughout this book, making adjustments as we move between the divine origins of sainthood and the creative hitching of sanctity to the immediate emotional, intellectual, and institutional needs of the faithful. Chapter 2 will consider the origins of sainthood in the landscape of the early church.

2

Inventing the Saints

Sainthood took on its most familiar forms from the death of Jesus *c.*33 CE to the decades following the Council of Chalcedon in 451 CE. At the beginning of this period, we might imagine Christianity as an inchoate, diffusely organized set of parallel experiments into the problem of how to live a good life, each working with a different mix of philosophical, religious, and linguistic heritages, but commonly inspired by a charismatic itinerant preacher and his disciples. Some of these experiments failed to take hold or continued along divergent paths, others were seen off by concerted attempts to build a church hierarchy that set boundaries in areas of belief and practice. By the end of the fourth century Christianity had forged a robust identity distinct from Judaism, and from various traditions of thought and practice designated heretical (for example Gnosticism and Donatism). Its newly closed canon of sacred texts, the Holy Bible, included the Hebrew Bible (the Old Testament) and a series of letters and biographies, parables and prophecies, poetry and revelation. It had attracted in large numbers the finest pagan intellects of the age and absorbed their learning, including Greek philosophy, Latin literary forms, and bodily practices. After suffering a period of intermittent persecution in the second and third centuries it secured political protection and vast material resources from Roman emperors and their imperial aristocracies sufficient to establish an institutional matrix spanning the whole of the Roman Empire. This was the Roman Catholic Church that from the mid-third century had begun to claim universal (*catholice*), apostolic authority derived from Jesus's chief disciple, St Peter.

Beyond the Roman frontier, in Armenia–Iberia (at that time a region between the Black Sea and the Caspian Sea), and Ethiopia, Christian communities enjoyed similar state tolerance to that given by imperial Rome. But others in Persia (modern Syria, Iraq, and Iran) continued to be severely persecuted for long afterwards, and some even fled further east to India and as far as China. The divergent political experiences of these communities, and their refusal at the Council of Chalcedon to accept a doctrinal settlement on the question of the Trinity imposed by an imperial Catholic Church, led to the great consolidations of what would ultimately become the Coptic, the Syriac, and Eastern Christian Churches.

Saints were at work in all these churches. But who among these diverse communities were saints? In what kind of life was Christian sainthood manifest? Through book learning, the spirit, bodily discipline, voluntary sacrifice? As prophet, teacher, healer, ascetic, martyr, philosopher, confessor, or virgin? Their vocations might vary but the holiness of saints came from their proximity to the source of all Holiness, God, and to his son, Jesus Christ of Nazareth, both Hebrew God Incarnate and Resurrection man.

A Community of Saints

The Christian church of the first and second centuries CE was an urban diaspora spread around the Mediterranean littoral, Hispania, Gaul, Asia Minor, North Africa, and Palestine. Jewish families and communities in Jerusalem, and those areas of Palestine where Jesus and his disciples had conducted their ministry were gradually joined by gentile converts to Christianity. Christian worship and association were broadly based around three elements: first the recognition of Jesus as the 'anointed one' (Hebrew, Messiah, Greek *Christos*); secondly, an apocalyptic expectation of Christ's imminent return; and thirdly, membership of a moral community steeped in a radical understanding of charity.

We are accustomed today to think of saints as being exceptional individuals made by the Church. Before that could happen the Church had to make itself. Christianity was a church of people from all kinds of backgrounds, of apostolic mission, of prophecy, and of witness, before it was a church of priestly hierarchy and territorial administration. The doctrine of papal primacy had obscure origins and contested validity. It arises from a passage in the Gospel, Matthew 16.18, sometimes known as the Petrine commission, 'And I say unto thee, thou art Peter, and upon this rock I will build my Church'. And upon this pun (Greek *Petros*, Peter, and *petra*, rock) the Roman Catholic Church built the notion of apostolic primacy, Peter the first Pope, granted by Christ the power 'to bind and loose' (i.e. an earthly jurisdiction sanctioned by heaven). Whilst it appears in the writings of Clement, Peter's successor, apostolic authority also applied to the successors of the other apostles in places like Alexandria and Antioch, and eventually sanctioned the ministry of bishops everywhere. The earliest types of saint were apostles. But they were also the faithful themselves, who were 'sanctified' through their common associations with Jesus Christ.

St Paul

The Greek word for saint (*hagios*) appears earliest and most frequently in the epistles (or missionary letters) of St Paul, who used it to denote *all* those baptized as Christians who made up the church. Originally a Greek-speaking Jewish tent-maker, Saul of Tarsus, the man who was later to become St Paul, holds perhaps the greatest claim to being the inventor of Christianity. Paul's epistles to the faithful of various cities (including Corinth, Philippi, Rome, and Ephesus) were written before the New Testament Gospels within a generation of the death of Jesus between *c.*30 and 60 CE. These and his missionary journeys, documented almost a century later in the *Book of Acts*, reveal a figure toiling to bring Christians of Jewish heritage into harmony with gentile converts on the meaning of Jesus's life and ministry and its implications for Christian religious observance.

Paul was the most prominent early advocate of the rather surprising idea that Jesus was a God-man. Not all early Christians accepted this, and many who did were in persistent disagreement over how that could possibly be so. Paul's endorsement of Jesus as God Incarnate is important for our understanding of early ideas of Christian sainthood. For

Paul, to be a saint was to be someone sanctified, or made holy through baptism. He used the term to address Christian communities as 'holy ones': 'to all in Rome who are loved by God and called to be saints, Grace and peace to you... To the church of God in Corinth, to those sanctified in Christ Jesus and called to be holy... To the saints in Ephesus, the faithful in Christ Jesus'. Baptism was a rite of sanctification 'in Christ' that separated its initiates from the world and conferred on them an indelible status and proximity through Christ to God, the source of all holiness. The first Christian communities can be seen in this way as groups apart from the rest of society, as saints.

We can drop in on one particular community of saints thanks to the archaeological time capsule that is the remains of a Christian house church in Dura-Europos, excavated in the 1930s by American archaeologists. Third century Dura-Europos was a frontier trading-town between Rome and Persia and home to several religious communities. In addition to temples to various Greek and oriental gods, a synagogue, and a Christian house church survive as private dwellings adapted for worship. We owe their survival in remarkably good condition to Roman-engineered siege works that filled in these buildings in anticipation of a Persian attack.

The arrangement of space in the house church offers clues to the priorities of Christian worship there. The main chamber of the church is aligned liturgically east to west. There is no obvious hierarchical ordering of space, however, no evidence of an altar, or any depiction among the church's wall paintings of a Christ figure, or saintly dedicatee, that

Figure 2 Baptistery at House Church of Dura-Europos: a sanctifying chamber.

become conventional in Christian churches (*basilicae*) a century later. The more important, if smaller, room was the baptistery, an initiation chamber of some spatial and visual sophistication, dedicated to sanctifying humans by bringing them closer to God through Christ. More expense and attention was focused on the baptistery (see Figure 2) than on the assembly chamber, reflecting its important function. In the spatial arrangement of the monumental font and wall paintings unfolds a sequence of stories familiar to us from the bible including the three Marys at the tomb, David and Goliath, and The Good Shepherd. These images helped effect the sacrament of baptism and

13

concentrate its meanings for catechumens (initiate Christians) preparing to undergo immersion, anointment, and Christian rebirth or, in Pauline terms, sanctification.

The Lives of the Early Saints

Christian churches included Jews and gentiles of Hellenistic culture, men and women of diverse social backgrounds, occupations, and status, urban colonies of mutual support groups holding each other to strict forms of moral conduct, all of them inspired by the Holy Spirit in anticipation of the Second Coming of Christ. The everyday challenge for these people was to overcome their social prejudices and avoid pecking orders that might exclude potential converts and fragment the community.

Paul's letters include invaluable moral advice on the avoidance of internal division through appeals to charity (Latin *caritas*), not the simple donation of money to good causes but the practice of loving one's neighbour as one loves God. A text from Paul's letter to the Corinthians (13:2–3), a favourite reading at wedding services today, stresses the vital pulse of these saintly communities: 'And though I have the gift of prophecy, and understand all mysteries, and all knowledge; and though I have all faith, so that I could remove mountains, and have not charity, I am nothing. And though I bestow all my goods to feed the poor, and though I give my body to be burned, and have not charity, it profiteth me nothing.'

A conviction among these Christian communities that end times were imminent underlined the need for outreach and knitted them together in mutual care and discipline. An early guidebook to church organization, the *Didache*, counselled Christians to keep high moral standards, to be open to the influence of holy faces among the community, to be unimpressed by status, and motivated not by money but by wisdom and charity. Early Christians would be led by an *episcopus* ('watchman' in Greek). Along with presbyters and deacons, these *episcopi* (or bishops) were charged with looking after their congregations and guiding them in the prayers and rites of the church. More like a team of supervisors or foremen than an executive board, nevertheless in churches like Rome, Antioch, Jerusalem, and Alexandria, these offices might enjoy power and wealth to be coveted. The *Didache* states that bishops and other ministers were to be 'of meek disposition and unattached to money', were to be selected by the community, and that masters were not to chastise servants since both shared common subjection to God's will.

Charitable relief of the poor and widows, the provision of burial services for the dead, and hospitality for itinerant teachers and prophets, all distinguished Christian communities from their neighbours. Many early Christians were tradesmen, artisans, or merchants with mobile wealth and professional, clerical, or artisanal talents, whose livelihoods depended upon mobility and networking. But their pragmatic sense of finance, contract, legal and social status was to be used to serve a greater, shared sense of moral accountability. The measures outlined in the *Didache* were designed to encourage fellowship among Christians in the face of inequalities and misfortunes, by insisting on the imminence of an overriding revelation that would judge individuals by means of the Holy Spirit, not worldly tokens of status and power. To be a 'saint' in the early church was no easily worn entitlement; it entailed commitment to self-discipline and the mutual monitoring of personal conduct or ethos, just as strictly as and certainly more intimately than that of later ecclesiastical institutions.

But individuals inevitably distinguished themselves as teachers, bishops, and prophets sufficiently to raise suspicion that greater talents indicated greater degrees of proximity to holiness. The balance of esteem in which bishops and prophets were held, for example, appears at times to have weighed in favour of the latter. The *Didache* reminds its readers to be just as supportive of their bishops, deacons, and presbyters as they were charitable to visiting prophets. The charisma, or divinely-conferred grace, in the ministry of these itinerant teachers posed a real danger that Paul's Christian message might be usurped and diverted. A good example of this was Montanism, a charismatic Christian movement of late second-century Phrygia, a province of Asia Minor. Its embrace of the Holy Spirit, of prophecy and revelation made adherents like Montanus, and his female acolytes, Prisca and Maximilla, early contenders for a new category of sainthood that elevated them above Paul's notion of the community of saints. The *Didache* was mindful of this danger, advising that if visiting prophets stayed for more than two days or asked for money rather than food, then they were to be deemed false. Prophecy was to become a qualification for sanctity subsumed among others (asceticism, pastoral care) within forms of holy life stabilized by monastic rules and institutions.

As it happened, it was neither the prophets nor the ecclesiastical officials of the church who first emerged with greater holy esteem from among these communities of the sanctified. The martyrs, witnesses to the faith to the point of death and often Christians from humbler backgrounds, were to do that.

Persecution and Martyrdom

The first Christian martyr was Stephen, a Hellenized Jew stoned in 35 CE by his own community for publicly claiming the righteousness of Jesus Christ. St Stephen the Protomartyr is untypical of most early martyrs. Most martyrs of the early church bore witness to Christ's message before persecuting authorities, enduring judicial torture and execution, often by being burned or fed to wild animals as a public spectacle. A distinction should be made between historical early martyrdoms and their later commemoration in the fourth-century cult of martyrs' relics. So much of what we know about the former is preserved in traditions invented in the latter period. Martyrdom was diverse in meaning and politically more complicated than those later traditions would have us believe.

Early Christian Martyrdoms

The Roman authorities were not determined to destroy Christianity, nor did Christian communities harbour insurrectionary ambitions. General persecutions occurred only briefly in the reigns of Decius (250–51), Valerius (257–60), and Diocletian (303–11), for little more than twelve years of the entire first three centuries of Christian history. Roman and provincial ruling elites regarded Christians with curiosity as a quaint oriental cult, only occasionally as a nuisance and threat to social order. But the novelty of Christian rituals, Christians' refusal when required publicly to burn incense in honour of traditional gods, and their growing number and cohesion in the third century made them vulnerable to scapegoating, a temptation Emperor Nero had been unable to resist as early as 64 CE. After a fire destroyed much of Rome he blamed the Christian population of the capital to deflect accusations of arson from himself.

A collection of correspondence between the Emperor Trajan (98–117 CE) and the provincial governor of Bithynia, Pliny the Younger, illustrates the improvised official treatment Christians typically received within a century of Jesus's death. In a letter of c.112 Pliny described in detail his troubles with Christians in the towns and surrounding villages. The impression is that Pliny was intervening to dampen down a popular witch-hunt. Public accusations of criminality and deviancy (the early Christians were sometimes accused of incest and cannibalism) and an anonymous pamphlet that listed individuals associated with Christian networks had clogged his court with cases. He sought guidance from Trajan on the legal status of his Christians and by what process they were to be tried. He doubted whether being a Christian automatically implied criminality, he was dubious about the credibility of their alleged crimes, and he acquitted those who offered incense and wine at the imperial altars on the grounds that no Christian would willingly make such an offering. After torturing two deaconesses he assured himself Christian beliefs were no threat to his office. As a gesture, however, he had executed those non-Roman townsfolk who under interrogation obstinately asserted their Christianity. But still the popular accusations necessitated his letter.

That persecution might often proceed from local tensions between Christians and their neighbours and not primarily from over-zealous authorities is supported by the death of forty-eight Christians in Lyon in 177 at the instigation of a mob. A letter of *c.*190 gives an account of this episode in which the citizens of Lyon turned against the city's colony of Greek Christians. The heroine of the story is Blandina, the servant of a mistress whose name is now lost. The author was clearly struck by the fact of her lowly status and female weakness, making her a powerful rhetorical illustration of the humble risen to glory. Like a 'noble athlete', Blandina wore her torturers out with the beatings she withstood, and after comforting her companions as each met their fate, she 'put on Christ' in submission on her own terms to the final cruel indignity of being tossed and gored to death by an enraged bull. Figure 3 is a highly dramatized evocation of the imminent fate of a group of Christian martyrs at an imaginary Roman venue that its painter, Jean-Léon Gérôme (d.1904), concocted from known Greek and Roman locations.

The account of the martyrdoms of Perpetua and Felicitas is a remarkable document combining the report of an execution of Christians that happened in Carthage in 202 with the prison diary of a martyr involved in it. Perpetua was a

Figure 3 Jean-Léon Gérôme (French, 1824–1904), *The Christian Martyrs' Last Prayer*.

22-year-old mother from a small-town, patrician family near Carthage. The diary is every bit as compelling and unpredictable as any scholar might expect of the rare first person account of an ancient female Christian in such extreme circumstances. Even if it has been tampered with in parts, perhaps to infuse the text with Montanist theology, Perpetua's voice is distinct and vivid in the sequence of painful encounters it portrays with her father, her experiences of incarceration and isolation from the baby she was still nursing, in the visions it recounts of an unbaptized dead brother Dinocrates saved nevertheless by her prayers, and of a fight she has *as a man* with an Egyptian in the arena in the days running up to her execution. Her obstinate defiance of the Roman magistrate, Hilarianus, feels like small change next to the sacrifices she steeled herself to in abandoning her baby and publicly defying her father. These themes have an emotional jaggedness that tears through even modern sensibilities.

Meanings of Martyrdom

Christian authors greeted the dreadful spectacle of martyrdom and the resounding celebrity it gave some of obscure background with ambivalence. Tertullian (d.240), the African theologian known for his robust oratory and rigorous moral discipline, regarded martyrdom as an endurance event like the marathon. His populist view of its significance is preserved in his *Ad martyras* (written *c*.190), which praises these athletes for feeding Christian ambition: 'the blood of the martyrs is the seed of the Church'. On the other hand, another African theologian, Origen (d.254), shared an antipathy for the melodrama of the martyr's path with pagan philosophers like Emperor Marcus Aurelius (161–80 CE) who preferred the noble suicide of Socrates. For the maidservant Blandina to display such indecorous stoicism undermined familiar social distinctions and strained good literary taste. Those interpreters of Christian scripture known as Gnostics were similarly unimpressed with martyrdom, regarding the body as of so little significance as to render its sacrifice a pathetic gesture. Martyrs' bodies could be described figuratively as treasure and precious gems, or as Eucharistic bread crushed between millstones. But the veneration of Bishop Polycarp of Smyrna's (d.155) incinerated remains on the birthday of his martyrdom (*dies natalis*) was an isolated early example of the cult of martyrs' relics, which really only took off in the fourth century.

There were reservations about those who deliberately sought martyrdom, and as persecution subsided in the Christian West so alternative paths to sainthood were imagined as metaphorical forms of martyrdom. Asceticism, virginity, or responsible office-holding as a 'confessor' to the faith, and intellectual endeavour became martyrdoms of a sort. Wisdom was valued above willingness to die for the cause and there were those who pointed to biblical precedents (for example, the flight to Egypt story) for the virtue of living to fight another day.

Fourth-century Christian Martyrdom: The Ecstasy and the Agony

Between 300 and 500 martyr-sainthood came to play an important part in a series of momentous changes in relations between political and religious authorities. During the second half of the period the Roman world gradually became administratively unhinged from its ancient capital in a process of transformation that saw new connections and movements forged between regions within and beyond the empire. In the West, Christianity came to dominate the ethnic polities known as kingdoms that formed out of the political accommodations reached between imperial aristocracies and displaced barbarian warriors and people.

During the fourth century, what would survive as the Eastern Roman or Byzantine Empire reconfigured itself around Constantinople, the new Rome its eponymous emperor began building *c.*330, and around the figure of the divinely ordained emperor. The 'Triumph of the Christian Church' is the traditional version of these events. According to this story Christianity survived state persecution, which officially ended with the Edict of Milan in 313, and then won, first, the toleration of Emperor Constantine (306–37), and then his establishment of Christianity as the imperial religion. The 'Church triumphant' and its emperor-architect, Constantine, had their official historian and panegyrist in Eusebius, bishop of Caesaria (313–39). Eusebius's popular vision of the fourth-century Church saw Constantine as the vessel of a greater divine plan at the public heart of which local memories of martyrdom pre-eminently featured. In his *Ecclesiastical History* Eusebius recorded and embellished all the local testimonies of martyrdom he could find and bequeathed to his successors an elaborate geography of places made holy by the presence of martyrs' remains.

In accounts of the glory of the martyrs were merged vivid devotional and historical truths that connected martyr-saints in heaven with their earthly audiences. Physical memorabilia and bodily remains became powerful means by which Christians attuned themselves to the heavenly presence (*praesentia*) of the saints. Inspired by Eusebius, churchmen translated relics to new architectural settings, produced epigraphy (inscriptions on public monuments), history, liturgy, and hagiography, preserving in them traces of eyewitness testimony and historical detail concerning early martyrdom but reframing and reworking them to suit the Church Triumphant theme. Pope Damasus (366–84) trawled the catacombs of Rome for the relics of Christian martyrs, incorporating them into its civic redevelopment. New public monuments in marble and mosaic were built, liturgical objects made, and commemorative events devised, all adorned and accompanied with verse inscriptions combining Christian holiness with Latin literary finesse. Rulers in Constantinople, the Christian capital *de novo*, quickly assembled an arsenal of saints' relics to rival that of Rome.

By the beginning of the fifth century the Holy Land became the ultimate destination for Christian pilgrimage. Constantine had the Church of the Holy Sepulchre built over the sites of Christ's crucifixion and resurrection, and stories of his mother Helena's discovery of the True Cross (upon which Christ was crucified) cemented the relationship between imperial authority and the Christian holy landscape. Bishops across the empire translated the remains of saints from cemeteries on the margins of their cities to downtown basilicas, rolling out networks between distant Christian communities, and opening new points of access to the prospect of heavenly mediation that saintly *praesentia* offered. The distribution of relics between leading churchmen further thickened imperial Christian networks. Damasus sent relics of St Paul, St Peter, and St Lawrence to Ambrose, bishop of Milan. Ambrose had the relics of St Gervase and St Protase translated into his newly built cathedral in 386 and sent fragments of their relics to Bishop Victricius of Rouen.

Like all evocations of history as destiny, the fourth-century story of the triumph of the Christian Church through the glory of its martyrs put the past to use in legitimizing a particular understanding of the present. A glance at two Christian communities for whom this story had no relevance will allow us to appreciate the historically contingent nature of this formative period in the history of sainthood.

Eastern Christians in Persia

It is technically inaccurate to claim that the fourth-century persecution of all Christians ended in 313. The triumph of the imperial Church brought no benefit to Christians living beyond the Roman frontier in Persia. In 325, the year of the First Nicene Council, convened to establish doctrinal unity across the imperial church, Constantine sent a letter to the Persian emperor, Shapur II (309–79), claiming to speak as protector of Christian communities in the Sasanian Empire. This placed the Christian churches in Persia in a vulnerable position given old enmities between these two empires and Shapur's revived territorial ambitions in the buffer state of (Christian) Armenia. After a military set back in Nisibus in 340, Shapur commanded taxes and religious obeisance to Zoroastrianism from the Christians led by Bishop Simeon bar Sebba'e of Ctesiphon. When neither materialized he unleashed savage persecution of Christians in Mesopotamia which lasted until 383, through his reign and that of his brother Ardashir II.

When they came to attend their first synod in 410 in Ctesiphon the Sasanian Christians were trapped on the wrong side of tectonic shifts in the geopolitics of the Mediterranean and Near East. They had only persecution to look back on in the fourth century, and no emperor protector like Constantine under whom to build their church. Instead they had a separate martyr heritage, first documented in a *martyrion* of 411 listing those executed under Shapur and Ardashir, and doctrinal differences detaching them from what would become the Catholic and Orthodox Churches of Byzantium and the Medieval West. The absence of imperial tolerance meant the future for Sasanian Christians would lie in their dispersal across a vast space from the eastern Mediterranean to South Asia and as far as China. St Thomas the Apostle became an important founding figure for those of them who made it to India.

Donatism

Martyrdom is—almost—the ultimate persuasive resort. I say almost because its success actually depends upon the continuing assertion of its bludgeoning logic by surviving sympathizers. Among communities with mixed sympathies martyrdom could test as well as cement solidarities. Whilst the Christian community persecuted in Lyon in 177 tolerated those who dodged martyrdom, in the wake of the Diocletian persecutions in North Africa, the veneration of martyrs became a bone of contention over who had the right to call themselves Christians. A section of its ecclesiastical elite could not forgive those it called *traditores*, who had 'handed over'—or like Bishop Caecilian of Carthage, been ordained by those who had handed over—sacred texts for burning during the persecutions. They cherished the tradition of an African church untainted by compromisers, made their own appointments to office, and built rural chapels known as *memoriae* where they venerated the relics of their martyrs.

They are known to history as Donatist heretics (after Donatus, one of their leading churchmen), a label their Catholic adversaries made to stick only after several decades of bitter rhetorical and legal attrition involving inflammatory sermonizing and violence on both sides. If we think of Donatism as a stereotype more than a heresy, and there is little evidence that the word had native meaning to those tarred with it, then martyrdom was a contested rather than a glorious feature of the story of the Church Triumphant in North Africa.

The Catholic Church's demonization of migrant agricultural labourers who travelled around the rural cells containing martyr-shrines suggests that Donatism had serious grassroots appeal. Its association of these, the *circumcellions* (Latin 'ones who move around cells'), with insurrectionary violence, gave the Catholic hierarchy leverage to co-opt state apparatus in its suppression of Donatism. Bishop Augustine of Hippo might well have nursed a lingering headache but perhaps also a grudging respect for the popularity of the Donatist martyr-shrines in his diocese. In later life, Augustine's Neoplatonic scepticism for the cult of martyrs' relics softened in response to the celebrated discovery in 415 of the relics of St Stephen the Protomartyr. It may also have reflected his observations of Donatist religious devotion to relics.

Asceticism, Monasticism, and Eremeticism

New saints of this era were no longer martyrs but predominantly ascetics. Asceticism was simultaneously a form of spiritual wrestling with the libidinous body and demonic temptation and a way of presenting oneself persuasively before a public audience *through* the body that had roots in Greek stoicism, the eastern traditions of the holy man, and Jewish communal life. The ancient Stoics and Platonists prized moderation, restraint, and command of the emotions as the way to a virtuous state of apathy (Greek *apatheia*; our 'apathy' today in learning classical Greek often obscures this pristine connotation of the word). Epictetus, the second-century Greek stoic and contemporary of Pope Clement I, used the word *askesis* (Greek 'self-discipline') to describe the means by which elite men of leisure (Latin *otium*, from which is derived our 'otiose') might achieve these goals. Christian ascetics drew on these ideas of athleticism and stoicism as a means of making visible the experience of holy intimacy with God. They followed biblical cues to 'sell your possessions and give to the poor' (Luke 12.33). Ascetics eschewed marriage and observed celibacy, bathed in cold water, fasted and abstained from meat, undertook flagellation, prayer, and vigil, and renounced property, social privilege, and material comforts. Signs of ascetic accomplishment included being granted visions and prophecies, communing with wild animals, or with divine permission, healing or performing miracles.

The eighteenth-century gentleman scholar Edward Gibbon famously saw asceticism as a retreat of the Roman elite from their ruling responsibilities that brought fatal consequences for the empire. However, quite the opposite appears more likely. Monasticism and other ascetic forms of sainthood represented a positive response to the contraction of administrative authority at regional and local levels, providing the source for much needed new forms of leadership and institutional organization. Christian asceticism was defined in a famous article by Peter Brown as 'the long drawn out, solemn ritual of dissociation—of becoming the total stranger'. But fourth-century ascetics opened divides *within* Christianity that stimulated renewed discussion and exchange between those compromised by the responsibilities of newly acquired ecclesiastical authority, and those who fixed their desires and ambitions on God alone. Out of these discussions emerged forms and understandings of leadership that had otherwise been absent in a religion whose founder had neither sought nor achieved earthly authority.

The main streams through which ascetic authority flowed came to be described as coenobitical (i.e. communal or monastic), or eremitical (solitary, reclusive). But these streams were fed by tributaries of ascetic practices that emerged out of local contexts, whether the mountain villages of Syria and Turkey, the deserts of Egypt, or in private places of seclusion in the cities of Italy, Gaul, and North Africa.

Stylites, Fools, and Hermits

One of the more eccentric of these practices, first associated with Simeon the Stylite (390–459), was pillar dwelling. Simeon spent almost forty years living at the top of a pillar situated on a ridge above the main trade route between Antioch and Aleppo. Among his imitators was Daniel, who pursued his prayers and vigils at the top of a pillar on the outskirts of Constantinople. Emperors visited both Simeon and Daniel, keen to associate with these famous holy specialists and perhaps even win their blessing in matters of church and state. With its curious resemblance to a 1980s platform style computer game, Figure 4 illustrates a monk ascending a ladder for a spiritual consultation with an unknown stylite, his censer stimulating the Holy Spirit to descend upon them both.

The holy fool represented another extreme form of that paradoxically detached engagement of the ascetic in society. In addition to the charity he dispensed, and the healings he performed, under the stigma of poor mental health, the

Figure 4 Basalt relief of Syrian stylite, fifth century.

sixth-century misfit St Symeon of Emesa conducted a campaign of personal moral reform in the communities he lived among. His *Vita* ('Life') describes how Symeon dragged a dead dog around the town, cultivated funny walks and odd gestures, threw nuts at women, and made a general nuisance of himself by upsetting traders' tables and publicly accusing people of sin. The impression is of a cross between the Jesus of the Gospels and Diogenes, the celebrated Greek philosopher who lived in a ceramic jar in the marketplace and carried a lantern around in broad daylight declaring he was looking for an honest man.

Reclusion was practised in the early church though we know very little of what it entailed. Some late and exiguous evidence exists for wandering recluses in the mountains of third-century Syria, called *boskoi* (Greek for 'grazers') on account of their foraging for nourishment from wild plants. The Sons and Daughters of the Covenant were another early Syrian ascetic movement we know very little about, but who appear to have been teacher-ascetics dwelling among Christian communities as *Ihidaya* (Syriac, meaning 'single, solitary ones'). These early Syrian traditions were eclipsed by those of the desert hermits of Egypt. Not the first but certainly the most famous of this movement, thanks to his *Vita*, written *c.*360 by Athanasius, bishop of Alexandria, was St Antony (d.356).

St Antony

Antony belonged to a well-off farming family. One day he heard Matthew 19.21 read in church: 'if you wish to be

31

perfect sell all your property, and give to the poor, then you will have treasure in heaven'. When his father died and he came into his inheritance, he renounced his wealth, sent his sister to a nunnery, and retreated to a local community of older male renouncers. In stages he moved from the city to the remote desert, taking up home in a fort abandoned by all but the demons with which he battled for most of his time in the wilderness. Athanasius's *Life* recounts the temptations Antony faced (a type of tribulation that echoes Tertullian's descriptions of martyrs in their prison cells), his dealings with the many visitors who came seeking his advice and cures, his run-ins with philosophers and besting of their reason with his simple faith, and his speaking of truth to power (Greek *parrhesia*) in the cause of Athanasius's orthodox theology.

The *Life of Antony* immediately became the most resounding model of Christian holy biography (ironically, given its appropriation of literary commonplaces from the anti-Christian polemicist, Porphyry's biography of Plotinus). St Augustine, seen as a father of the Roman Catholic Church, was one of those classically educated young men who read a Latin translation of it and converted. It went east and was translated into Syriac. After a lengthy sojourn in the Egyptian deserts John Cassian (365–435) took the *Life* west to Southern Gaul where he became an interpreter of the Egyptian tradition to the hermits and monks experimenting with asceticism in the Lérins Islands and Marseille. He founded an abbey there dedicated to St Victor, the third-century martyred Roman soldier. John Cassian invested the Greek ideas of apathy he had encountered in the desert with a Christian language of purity of spirit and heart. Other literary formulations of Christian spirituality arose out of the ascetic experiment including the sayings of the desert fathers (Greek *apothegmata*), and such practical guidance offered by the monk Evagrius Ponticus (345–99) as how to spot the work of demons, how to guard against the chief temptations, and how to advance in the knowledge of God.

Monks

Asceticism had social, ethical, and spiritual dimensions that in some circumstances might conflict. The path to spiritual perfection could easily become the high road to pride. And how far did the monastic renunciation of society represent sectarian exclusivity rather than moral engagement with the ordinary faithful? The monastic Rule (Latin *Regula*) legislated for these matters. It took as its biblical precedent a passage from the Acts of the Apostles (Acts 2.44–5): 'all the believers were together and had everything in common. Selling their possessions and goods, they gave to anyone as he had need.' The monastic experiment took off in the late third century. The soldier St Pachomius (292–348) brought his military rigour to the role of abbot of one of the earliest Christian monasteries, in his native Upper Egypt. Along with Antony, he is particularly venerated by the Coptic Christians. St Basil visited the Pachomian communities and later, as bishop of Caesarea, instituted his own monastic precepts in Asia Minor. In addition to the Pachomian principle of seniority based upon time served rather than social status, Basil prized obedience to the abbot and humility and charity before one's companions in his interpretation of Acts.

Frumentius, Nino, Severinus, Patrick, and Martin

Saints could also be quite mobile in this period. They were often travellers, voluntary or otherwise: conscript soldiers, slaves, brides, and administrators, as well as traders, pilgrims, and miscellaneous vagrants. The transient, in-between status that travel conferred and the universal language of authority that Christianity now supplied allowed them to represent emerging local traditions of holy revelation in ways similar to the early church prophets. This is certainly the tidy impression we often receive later from monks, bishops, and biographers seeking to benefit from the commemoration of these figures.

Three examples are the traditions of St Frumentius, St Nino, and St Severinus. Rufinus of Aquileia, the early fifth-century Latin translator and continuator of Eusebius's *Ecclesiastical History*, preserved early knowledge about the first two. Frumentius was a captive Christian slave who made his way in the royal court of the kingdom of Axum. Ethiopian Axum controlled a strategic trading location from its port of Adulis on the Red Sea inland to Axum, linking inner East Africa to Arabia, and Egypt with the Indian Ocean. Frumentius persuaded the king, Ezana, to convert. The story goes on to explain how Frumentius returned to Axum and founded the Church there after travelling to Alexandria to receive his episcopal commission from Bishop Athanasius. Subsequent leaders of the Ethiopian Church were customarily appointed from Alexandria. St Nino (or Ninny), like Frumentius, was another Christian slave who found herself sold and transported along similarly important trading routes to the kingdom of Iberia–Georgia in the Caucuses. Iberia's royal court embraced Christianity when this Cappadocian slave girl and holy woman cured its queen and converted King Mirian III (d.361) after God, at Ninny's prayerful request, reversed his sudden loss of eyesight. The king sent to Constantine asking for priests and resources to establish his church. Almost a century later St Severinus of Noricum (d.482) was an Italian tourist among the Egyptian ascetics who eventually set himself up as an aid worker in a war-torn region of the Danube (in what is now modern Austria). The saint's relics were later translated to Naples where one of his followers, Eugippius, founded a monastery and went on to complete a version of the saint's life in 511.

Scholars are rightly cautious about whether these and similar stories preserve evidence of genuine roots in the past or are commemorative routes from the past invented later. No doubt some of them contain kernels of truth about real people. We stand on firmer ground with the evidence for the lives of St Patrick, the fifth-century apostle saint to Ireland, and St Martin, the fourth-century holy-man bishop. A British captive slave transported to Ireland some time in the mid-fifth century, Patrick is another example of the lowly, displaced Christian who converted kings. Two of his autobiographical works survive: the *Confessio* and the *Letter to King Coroticus* in which Patrick explains his mission to Ireland and defends himself against criticisms from other Christian groups. St Martin (316–97) was a Roman soldier from Pannonia (modern Hungary) who renounced his military commission to become a 'soldier of Christ' (*miles Christi*). He practised asceticism with St Hilary of Poitiers, in Gaul, before going on to found a monastery at Marmoutier and become bishop of Tours. Martin was the prototype of a peculiarly medieval western figure, the holy man parachuted into episcopal administration.

By the end of the fifth century the martyr, the ascetic, and the confessor had become the most important forms of Christian sainthood. The ascetic and the confessor-bishop brought invaluable skills of advocacy, literacy, and spectacle to the service of worldly authority embodied by the Christian kings, or 'little Constantines' of the early Medieval West. A predicament for bishops lay in balancing the judicial and ministerial duties of apostolic office with the claims made upon them by these kings and by their own family relations. In monasticism lay the ascetic means by which tensions between earthly and heavenly loyalties might be contained. Unsurprisingly then, the theme of the monk-bishop holding the Christian king to moral account recurs throughout the Middle Ages and beyond, though the establishment of papal canonization in the thirteenth century and the Reformation changed the rules of the game.

Let us see how this developed in the Middle Ages, the subject of Chapter 3.

3

Saints in the Middle Ages

After Empire and Before 'Europe', c.500–1000

The Church's triumphal collaboration with the Roman
Empire had ended by 500 CE. Under internal and external
pressure the empire's western provinces broke away from its
eastern half and came under the fragmented political control of Franks, Goths, Anglo-Saxons, and other migrant ethnic groupings. One of these successor kingdoms, Visigothic
Spain, was swept away by Arab-Islamic conquerors at the
beginning of the eighth century. The imperial church survived only in the Byzantine Empire, but it too lost important
provinces to Islam in the seventh and eighth centuries,
among them Jerusalem and the Holy Land. Political authority
hung on in the West through the accommodation reached
between two new forms of leadership, the holy man bishop
and the Christian king. Saints and their relics—venerated at
cathedrals, the court chapels of kings, and monasteries—
fostered a new civilization, Latin Christendom. It took on
different forms according to local conditions across the old
western Roman provinces and beyond them, deep into insular
Britain, east of the Rhine, and north into pagan Scandinavia.

We know most about saints' cults at Roman administrative and diocesan centres where highly literate provincial aristocracies continued to produce written and monumental traces of their devotion to saints. As imperial administration faded these urban elites found themselves among warriors, warlords, and their followers, and a rural population of *pagenses* or country folk. In these conditions they staked their wealth and literary talents on the status they could leverage from the heavenly support of saints. According to Robert Markus, their recruitment of holy men from places like the Île d'Yeu, the mountain forests of the Jura north of the western Alps, and the Lérin Islands of the French Riviera represented an 'ascetic invasion' of episcopal office. Holy insurgents like St Eucherius of Lyon (d.449), St Germanus of Auxerre (d.448), and St Caesarius of Arles (d.542) followed in the footsteps of St Martin, as traced by Sulpicius Severus in his biography of the saint, brokering power as missionaries, monastic founders, and bishops.

Gallo-Roman families bathed the memories of these holy figures in the pious wordings of hagiography, poetry, and epigraphy. The paternal family of Gregory, bishop of Tours (d.594), for example, was devoted to the cult of St Julian, a third-century martyr, most of whose remains rested at Brioude in the Auvergne (his head was buried with the body of St Ferréol in Vienne). On separate occasions, his father Florentius and his uncle Gallus went on pilgrimage to Julian's tomb in the Auvergne. Gregory's mother, Armentaria, was devoted to the cult of St Benignus of Dijon, whose relics had been discovered and enshrined by her grandfather, St Gregory, bishop of Langres (506–*c*.539).

Gregory's maternal uncle was St Nicetius, bishop of Lyon (552–73). A more distant ancestor, Vettius Apagathus, was one of the Lyon martyrs of 177. Gregory also avidly collected stories about the saints in his writings. In his *Ten Books of Histories* we hear of an archbishop of Trier who called a deacon-stylite down from his pillar on the edge of the city. The archbishop's intervention saved the deacon, known as St Walfroy, from the unforgiving climate of northern Europe. It was almost certainly also meant to prevent an ambitious young deacon from dazzling devotees with his eastern ascetic tricks at the expense of episcopal authority.

The fifth through to the seventh centuries in Gaul saw the development of centres of pilgrimage, devotional spaces, and the sanctoral cycle of feast days. Churches had originally been built over the crypts (*hypogea*) of martyrs, but bishops later staged ritual elevations of saints' remains to tombs before altars, or else to lavish structures behind them. People of all social backgrounds flocked to these shrines on feast days in the belief that saints could intercede for pilgrims who brought a gift, a prayer, and a public show of devotion. Records of miracles accumulated at their tombs showing how saints supported diocesan territories, or monastic estates, and protected communities from plague, famine, ill health, and injustice.

Criticism of Cult

All this *post mortem* activity of saints, associated with their relics, was troubling to Augustine and other churchmen. It brought the Incarnation and the Eucharistic sacrament into question as exclusive points of cosmic overlap between God and man. How could saints be present in heaven and active in the world? Did they share in the Godhead immediately at death? What exactly distinguished the souls of saints from those of the ordinary faithful after death, and could that distinction possibly be on a level with that of Jesus Christ? Did the saints act autonomously or were their miracles co-ordinated by God (and how did that work)? In this regard had saints now replaced the messenger role the Bible ascribed to angels? Did not the *post mortem* miracles of saints detract from the soteriological (concerning salvation) work the clergy conducted through the sacraments?

A practical urgency attached to these questions for Augustine, in whose diocese were countless tiny churches where the dust and rags of Donatist martyrs received daily veneration. As we have seen, he came round to the idea of relic veneration after the discovery of St Stephen the Protomartyr's relics. But his Gallic contemporary Vigilantius, whose views are indirectly preserved in Jerome's polemical pamphlet, *Against Vigilantius*, represented a section of the Gallo-Roman ecclesiastical elite similarly troubled by the cult of relics. They objected to the idea that dead saints could intervene in the lives of the living, to the practice of kissing 'dust and ashes wrapped in costly cloth', the use of relics to extort money for private gain, and to the opportunity nocturnal vigils provided for the conduct of illicit trysts. On the other hand, Bishop Victricius of Rouen gave a sermon, *In Praise of the Saints*, at his translation of the relics of Saints Gervase and Protase (sent him by Bishop Ambrose of Milan in 396). In it he outlandishly claimed that martyrs' relics 'by gift, not by property, by adoption not by nature' shared an immediate physical, spiritual, and blood unity with the Godhead.

The theory of saintly intercession was difficult for churchmen to reduce to simple doctrinal statements. To do so risked legislating for God's actions, perhaps even ventriloquizing his intentions. Nevertheless, as saints' cults became endemic in the medieval West, some guidance was urgently needed. Pope (and St) Gregory the Great (d.604) was an important shaper of the language used to talk about the veneration of relics and other sacred objects. As its title suggests, his *Dialogues on the Miracles of the Italian Fathers*, written *c.*593–4, featured a conversation between Gregory and his pupil, a Roman deacon named Peter, at the heart of its rhetorical exposition. Gregory used this 'FAQ format' to debate eschatological and pastoral issues affecting Christianity from the British Isles to Byzantium. He believed Judgement Day was imminent and moral leadership an urgent requirement to bring people to the faith. Readers of the *Dialogues* could be assured that saints performed miracles in life and after death, that they did so with humility in knowing that they had been authorized by God, that miracles were not ends in themselves but aids to religious conversion and signs to help prepare the faithful for Judgement.

Gregory's views on moral leadership were articulated in his *Regula Pastoralis* (Pastoral Care), one of the most useful guides to the relationship between holiness and public authority ever written. His advice to St Augustine—the monk-missionary he sent to England to convert the Anglo-Saxons—against the vainglory that might accompany his gift of miracle working, comes straight from his playbook: 'if you remember that you have at any time sinned against our Creator, either by word or deed, always call it to mind, to the end that the remembrance of your guilt may crush the vanity which rises in your heart'.

Into the Fold

Pope Gregory's mission to the Anglo-Saxons brought a part of the empire lost to paganism back under the pastoral care provided by the gifts of Christian monasticism, holy leadership, and literacy. Christian Roman Britain has survived in little more than Brittonic place names hinting at generations of early saints in Wales, Cornwall, and pockets of the old Roman province. Only one of these, St Alban, the third-century soldier-martyr, is better known thanks to his inclusion in the *Ecclesiastical History of the English People* written by the eighth-century Northumbrian monk-scholar Bede. The continuous history of England effectively begins with this book. It charts the missions of monk-saints to pagan kings and their peoples over several decades. The more visionary among the Anglo-Saxon kings seized upon the opportunities these holy patronage networks gave them to upgrade their authority and secure lucrative associations with continental kings. They welcomed, among others, St Augustine to Kent, St Paulinus to Northumbria, St Birinus to the West Country, and St Cedd and St Chad to the East and West Midlands.

Two major saints caught up in this drama were Cuthbert and Wilfrid. A 'pamphlet war', according to Alan Thacker, began over their legacies in the earliest known works of

English hagiography, dating to the first decades of the eighth century. These legacies concerned the organization of the Anglo-Saxon church. St Cuthbert (d.687) had been brought up in the Ionan monastic tradition of Melrose Abbey, but became convinced of Roman customs of worship (the wearing of the tonsure, and the calculation of Easter) after the synod of Whitby convened by Abbess Hilda in 664. His exemplary life as a hermit on the island of Farne graced him with the ability to communicate with wild animals, to prophesy death and the outcome of battles, and to heal. When he became bishop of Lindisfarne he travelled the more remote rural corners of his diocese by foot to minister to the laity. When the monks of Durham opened his tomb in 1104, they found his body to be incorrupt (see Figure 5).

St Wilfrid was a different kind of saint. An aristocratic Northumbrian courtier turned pilgrim to Rome, St Wilfrid converted to the religious life in the church of St Andrew, founded by Gregory the Great in the Caelian Hills. He travelled with an armed retinue, beguiled kings and queens into endowing monasteries, collected bishoprics, and accumulated a portfolio of churches so dispersed that it failed to survive his death as a going concern.

Monasticism proved so popular among the Irish *túatha* (petty kingdoms) that Hiberno-Latin hagiography predated the appearance of hagiography in England by almost half a century. The *Life of St Patrick* by Muirchú and the *Journey of St Patrick* by Bishop Tírechán, both of the second half of the seventh century, are propagandic appropriations of St Patrick's cult to serve an aggrandizing monastic confederacy centred on the church of Armagh. In Tírechán's

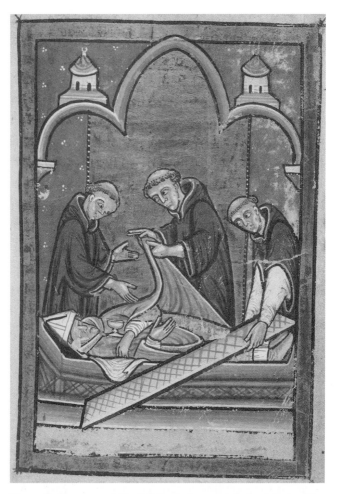

Figure 5 Discovery of St Cuthbert's incorrupt body, late twelfth-century ms. illustration, Yates Thomson, MS 26, f.77r., British Library.

account of Patrick's journey we are invited to witness Patrick's progress through an extensive Irish landscape as he founds churches and obliterates the druid priests who cross him. The details of Patrick's supposed fifth-century itinerary suspiciously resemble a list of places Armagh was targeting for takeover in the seventh century.

Iona was part of a different monastic confederacy (that had nurtured Cuthbert), the extension of an Irish clan system that linked Ulster to Pictland (modern Scotland) and was home from the mid-seventh century to Adomnán, who wrote the *Life of St Columba*. The *Life* is a rich collection of testimonies to the sanctity and miraculous powers of Columba, the founder of Iona, modelled on Evagrius's *Life of St Antony* and Sulpicius Severus's *Life of St Martin*. Irish monks were welcomed on the continent as wandering *peregrini*, or pilgrim exiles. Chief among them was St Columbanus (d.615), who led a party of Irish monks through Neustria (northern France), the Alpine regions of modern Switzerland, and northern Italy, founding monasteries as he travelled, most successfully at Luxeuil and Bobbio, where Jonas of Bobbio (d.659) was to write his *Vita*.

Frankia

Back on the continent, Frankish elites followed the Gallo-Roman tradition of bending saints' cults to their political ambitions. Monastic endowment, the sponsorship of cult, and control of relics represented a pious dimension of their strategies to secure land and power. There were winners and losers in this game. To the daughters and widows of aspiring dukes, kings, and lords came opportunities to renounce or survive marriage, and gain saintly status as virgins and abbesses. Losers included partisan churchmen assassinated by rival families or ruthless siblings, whose deaths were repackaged as martyr-cults for political gain. Almost half a dozen such bishops and abbot-martyrs on opposite sides of family feuds have been identified in seventh-century Frankia.

The phenomenon of martyred holy nobles cropped up elsewhere in later centuries. St Wenceslas (d.935), and the West Saxon prince, Edward the Martyr (d.978), were both murdered by brothers (the former becoming patron saint of Bohemia). Both brother successors moved quickly to contain the political opposition these assassinations fomented by presiding over their cults. In similar fashion, the Viking rulers of early ninth-century East Anglia issued a coin commemorating the death of St Edmund, the Anglo-Saxon king they had murdered only thirty or so years earlier.

A different opportunity for martyrdom transpired in Al-Andalus (Muslim Spain) among Cordoban martyrs of the 850s. Over fifty Christians there publicly defamed Muhammad and Islam, and refused to retract when challenged to do so. The surviving evidence suggests this was more than a simple clash of cultures. The priest Eulogius kept a record of the martyrdoms, the *Memorale Sanctorum*, and his friend, Paul Alvar, wrote his *Life* when he was also martyred. The martyrs were from families recently converted from Judaism, from mixed families of Muslim and Christian partnerships, or were apostate Muslims. In short they did not represent the entire Christian diaspora in Al-Andalus. Rather they were a particular community of

Christians roused by monastic anxieties about Christian assimilation to the language, literature, and culture of Muslim-Arab society. Similar patterns of acculturation had taken place among Eastern Christians in Syria by the end of the eighth century and began later, in early tenth-century Egypt.

Carolingian Reform of the Cult of Saints

The first great attempt to centralize and regulate the cult of saints was made by the Pippinids, a Frankish dynasty with imperial ambitions of the second half of the eighth century. The most famous of the Pippinids was Charles the Great, or Charlemagne, who ruled from 768 to 814. Charlemagne carved out an empire exceeding traditional Frankish boundaries, north to the frontiers of Scandinavia, east beyond the Rhine and up to the Elbe, and south through Aquitaine into Lombard Italy and across the Pyrenees. Crowned emperor by Pope Leo III in 800, Charlemagne was the biggest 'little Constantine' of the age. He ploughed the profits of conquest and plunder into an extensive network of monasteries committed to the renovation of classical and Christian learning and moral correction of the people. In the capitularies, or legal statements, issued periodically throughout his reign can be discerned a 'relic policy' designed to choke at birth local attempts to galvanize political will around new saints.

In the *Admonitio Generalis* issued in 789, and at the councils of Mainz of 811 and 813, the translation of saints' bodies without synodal or princely approval was prohibited, a universal list of official saints was produced, and cults were placed under episcopal management and records supporting them were made a requirement. Consequently, new cults became more difficult to invent, and though hagiographical production increased, it was focused on vintage saints, especially Roman martyrs, whose relics fetched up in Frankish monasteries via illicit traders working out of the catacombs of Rome.

The Byzantine Empire and the Eastern Churches

Saints were an important feature of religious life in the Byzantine Empire and in all the Eastern Christian Churches. These churches shared a common inheritance with the Latin West in many of the apostles, martyrs, ascetics, and Fathers of the early church. But new saints flourished in the different political and cultural conditions of the East, and, along with newly remembered old saints, attracted the devotion of emperors, the avowed religious, and the people.

The Coptic Christians of Egypt built their identity around St Mark the Evangelist, martyred in Alexandria in 68 CE. Important saints in Coptic Christianity were patriarchs of Alexandria such as St Athanasius (d.373), St Cyril (d.444), and St Dioscorus, who died in 454, in exiled opposition to the decrees of Chalcedon. In addition to Antony and Pachomius, the Copts venerate numerous representatives of their dense and rich monastic tradition, including St Shenouté the Archimandrite (d.466), abbot of the White Monastery near modern Sohag, and St Macarius (d.391), hermit and monk of the Wadi-al Natrun region, where a cluster of desert monasteries was famous for producing patriarchs and sheltering them in dangerous times. Eighth-century Coptic martyrologies drew upon exemplars from the early church to teach Christians to hold fast against the temptation to convert to Islam. The harsh taxes and occasional persecutions aimed at monasteries and Coptic communities by the Abbasid governors and Fatimid and Mamluk rulers, led to their depletion through death, conversion, and assimilation to Islam. But Muslims occasionally converted in the other direction, such as Al-Wadih ibn al-Raja', who was ordained a priest, and eventually became a saint. Among the continuing hardships of persecution, the looted churches, destroyed monasteries, and martyrdoms, the Copts are resiliently witness to their faith in Egypt and Libya even today.

Emperors and Saints

The special relationship between the ruler and the cult of saints and their relics was also unlike that in the West. Byzantine emperors were periodically challenged by external military threats from all directions, and by threats from rival dynasties if they wavered in their leadership. Constantinople, the almost impregnable walled city at the heart of the Empire, suffered the indignity of foreign incursions by land and sea into its provinces of Palestine, Syria, Egypt, Asia Minor, and parts of Italy and the Balkans. From the west and the north, first the Avars and then later the Slavs, the Bulgars, and the Rus were the threat. The Sasanians attacked from the east, until being swept away by Arab armies from the south, who dismembered the Byzantine Empire following the decisive battle of Yarmuk in 637. Of all these enemies, none proved as consequential as the crusaders of the Latin West who sacked Constantinople during the Fourth Crusade of 1204 and imposed an alien regime on the Greeks for most of the thirteenth century. During that time a large share of the city's relics, found in its churches and the imperial treasury, was confiscated or plundered, and redistributed to favoured churches in the West.

An instrument of Byzantine rule in these circumstances, no less important than military command and the management of material resources, was the authority emperors claimed in relation to God. The centralizing and unifying power of the emperor depended upon him enforcing his theocratic authority on the Orthodox Church, on the leading patriarchs of Constantinople, Alexandria, Jerusalem, and Antioch, and on those abbots and monks of its provincial monasteries, the seedbeds of learning, sanctity, and devotion to saints.

Constantinople's relic collection helped in this regard. It was an ideological arsenal that emperors could repeatedly deploy in their military campaigns. The earliest association of the imperial capital of Constantinople with a saintly patron was with St Helena, mother of the first Christian emperor, Constantine. Rufinus, a fifth-century Latin translator and continuator of Eusebius's *Ecclesiastical History*, narrated the story of Empress Helena's pilgrimage to Jerusalem in 326 and collection of relics, chief among them her discovery of the relic of the True Cross. By the mid-fifth century, Constantinople had acquired the robe of the Virgin Mary from pilgrims returning from the Holy Land.

The link between saints and imperial martial endeavour was strongly established during the sixth century under the rule of Justinian. In the first quarter of the seventh century, Byzantium found itself in an existential struggle with Persia. A particular low point was the capture of Jerusalem in 614, and the removal to Ctesiphon of that portion of the True Cross that had been kept there. The Emperor Heraclius was shrewd in treating this as a holy war. He used an image of Christ from Edessa known as the Mandylion to command his troops in Bithynia. At one crucial moment in 626, with Heraclius pressing the Persians in the East, the Avars and Persian armies attempted a joint siege of Constantinople. The 80,000-strong Avar army was prevented from ferrying the Persians over the Bosphorus, and repelled, after the procession of another image of Christ, the *Kamoulianai*, around the city walls, and when the Virgin Mary of the church of Blachernae was seen among the mayhem defending the city. The *Akathistos* (Greek 'without sitting'), a hymn to the Blessed Virgin, was written to commemorate the night-long standing vigil presided over by Sergius, patriarch of Constantinople, in request of her assistance. From 629, the emperor adopted the title of *basileus*, king-emperor, in imitation of the Old Testament royal title used by David. The following year, the True Cross was returned with great ceremony to Jerusalem. But no sooner was the Persian threat seen off than a catastrophic series of defeats saw Arab armies, united in Islam, take Palestine, Egypt, and other parts of North Africa—two thirds of Byzantine territory—from its rulers.

These protracted wars ensured that military saints were a feature of Byzantine devotional life. At its height in the fifth and sixth centuries, the cult of St Menas, soldier-martyr at Abu Minas, received enough far-travelled pilgrims to

Figure 6 An *ampulla* of St Menas, Abu Minas.

support a ceramics industry producing small terracotta flasks. These contained holy oil and water, and bore his name and image (see figure 6), some of them illustrating the story of obstinate camels who refused to move one way or the other, having brought him to the place of his cult. St Menas's military career was remembered in stories of his protection of Alexandria against the Bedouins, though unfortunately he failed to resist the Persians, who destroyed Abu Minas in 619.

St George was a Palestinian soldier-martyr of the third century. He appears in the *Martyrology* attributed to Jerome and was adopted as a patron of the Byzantine army in the fifth century. The Irish monk Adomnán recorded a late seventh-century Anglo-Saxon pilgrim to the Holy Land recounting the story of a soldier addressing a portrait of St George in conversation, asking him for protection on his imminent campaign.

St Demetrius was another soldier-martyr of the third century, venerated as patron-protector of the important Macedonian port city of Thessaloniki from at least the mid-fifth century. A seventh-century collection of his miracles, written as morale-boosting homilies for his congregation at the Hagios Demetrios (Cathedral of St Demetrius), recounts several historic defences Demetrius made of the city against the Slavs. The other warrior saints were: two martyrs named Theodore; Sergius and Bacchus; and the great field marshal (*archistrategos*) St Michael the archangel. Michael's angelic status made him unusual as a saint, but his role in the Book of Revelation in leading an army of angels against a dragon-like Satan meant that the Byzantine army especially revered him in the apocalyptically minded seventh century.

The Iconoclast Controversy

The reference to a soldier talking to an image of St George is an early example of devotion to religious icons, images of holy persons in which the essence of the person depicted was believed to be present. The earliest of these relic-images were thought to be *acheiropoieta* (objects made without human hand), a term that, among other things, prevented awkward discussion about the worship of graven images.

They seem exclusively to have depicted Jesus Christ. The seventh and eighth centuries saw a groundswell of popular devotion to icons, extending to the depiction of saints by artisans for churches and for private use. The burgeoning popular practice of icon veneration horrified some in the Orthodox Church, triggering an age of 'image struggles' punctuated by two periods of imperial-decreed iconoclasm, the first traditionally seen as 726 to 787, the second 815 to 843, ending with what became known as the Triumph of Orthodoxy.

Conservative churchmen did use imperial bans on icon veneration and the regulation of icons to destroy them and persecute their supporters, but iconoclasm was not as comprehensive as had once been thought. A collection of around forty icons at the monastery of St Catherine's, Sinai, including many dateable to this period, suggests that icon production was not curtailed everywhere. In fact, the counter-polemic could be lively and acerbic. At Easter 815, St Theodore the Studite, the iconophile abbot of the Studios, Constantinople, had his monks process through their gardens holding icons aloft for their powerful neighbours to see above the monastery's walls. The illustrator of the ninth-century Khludov Psalter of Constantinople famously juxtaposed the biblical image of Roman soldiers feeding the crucified Christ sour vinegar with a sponge on the end of a pole, with iconoclasts applying lime to an image of Christ painted on the wall. There were those who simply sought greater definition of the correct use of icons in worship and were concerned that the removal of religious portraiture from Orthodox churches represented 'Saracen-minded' acceptance of the idea that idolatry had brought God's wrath on the empire in the shape of Islam.

In fact Islam, with its strict rejection of human forms in sacred art, did not provoke iconoclastic thinking so much as it helped some Christians towards a clearer articulation of distinction on the issue. The Triumph of Orthodoxy in 843 embraced a theology of icon veneration grounded in the late seventh-century writings of Mansur Ibn Sarjun, an Arab Christian citizen of Damascus, who had served in the Umayyad Islamic court before entering the monastery of St Sabas near Jerusalem. St John of Damascus, as he is remembered in the Orthodox Church, was a Greek writer living in one of those Christian enclaves beyond the Roman frontier, and often (though not in the case of his Melchite community) beyond the theological dispensation of Chalcedonian Byzantium, as a resident of ambivalent status within the Dar al-Islam (the house of Islam). The clear definition of idolatry mattered to these communities because it helped in the assertion of communal and religious separation from Islam (considered a Christian heresy by theologians).

St John of Damascus argued that the representation of God and the saints was made perfectly acceptable by God's revelation of the divine presence in the Incarnation. Just as God had appeared in human form, something of the divine might exist in all matter (an idea developed from St Dionysius the Pseudo-Areopagite, a late fifth-century Syrian neoplatonist Christian who wrote as the early Athenian convert of St Paul mentioned in Acts). The issue became not whether but *how* icons should be venerated. The focus thus moved from the icon to the devotion of the faithful, and the proper forms it might take in the presence of different kinds of image.

The idea elegantly accommodated demotic religious devotions with the more ritual and pastoral interests of the Orthodox Church's priestly hierarchy. Thereafter these principles found expression in a new architectural configuration of Orthodox churches that combined the square on a circle structure, the reservation of liturgical space (the altar and relics) behind the iconostasis, a wall upon which icons were arranged programmatically, and religious portraiture distributed around the church interior. The effect was the recreation of a cosmic hierarchy with saints occupying the pavement level as if circulating among the congregation, and the apostles, Virgin Mary, and the angels elevating one's gaze up to an image of Christ the Pantocrator (All-mighty).

A New Voice and an Old Silence

The Triumph of Orthodoxy's willingness through the cult of saints to reach out to the laity found its ninth-century complement in the Greek Orthodox mission to the Slavic peoples of Moravia, Pannonia, and Bulgaria. Patriarch Photius of Constantinople directed Constantine (monastic name Cyril) and his brother Methodius to these frontier kingdoms on the western edge of the Byzantine Empire, which were simultaneously attracting the attentions of German missionaries and the Pope. Part of what decided the protracted contest between Rome and Constantinople over the souls of these peoples was the missionary approach of Saints Cyril and Methodius. One of Photius's finest scholars, St Cyril, adapted Greek letters to render the Slavic spoken language in a script that would be used to furnish its churches with sacred and liturgical texts. Its early form, Glagolitic, was eventually eclipsed by Cyrillic, which later became the sacred script of the Russian Orthodox Church.

The late tenth century saw the appearance, in the *Life of St Symeon the New Theologian*, of a new form of asceticism concerned with an 'inner stillness, or silence', directed towards *theosis*, or divine union with God. In the 970s St Symeon rejected his aristocratic family connections at the imperial court for the monastic life at the Studios under his spiritual mentor, St Symeon Eulabes. After keeping vigils and fasting, overcoming spiritual pride and demonic ambush, Symeon was rewarded with visions of the divine light: 'at the moment he prostrated himself before God, behold, he saw with his intellect a bright cloud descending upon him. It produced an exquisite pleasure and sweetness in his soul, filling it with divine grace...' Hesychasm, as it became known, would later flourish in thirteenth- and fourteenth-century Greek Orthodoxy, and in eighteenth-century Russian Orthodoxy.

Saints in Latin Christendom, *c.*1000–1500

The later Middle Ages saw developments in the cult of the saints in Latin Christendom. New religious orders and an increase in vernacular piety created new kinds of saint and forms of devotion. The relationship between church and state changed dramatically as a result of papal-led reformation, sustained from the mid-eleventh to the early thirteenth century. From the smallest parish to the greatest prince-bishopric, a gradual but at times fiercely fought campaign for clerical celibacy and against the sale of office slowly wrenched the church free of its entanglements with imperial, royal, and aristocratic patronage and privilege. Henceforth, the inheritance or purchase of priestly office was anathema, and bishops and priests were to be ordained and invested by fellow churchmen.

The liberty of the church had consequences for the cult of saints: it introduced greater ecclesiastical supervision of the relationship between saints and families of political importance. Monasticism remained an important institution, but became one among other forms of association, including crusading and pilgrimage, confraternities, universities, and patrician families, that nurtured and venerated saints in different languages, artistic media, rituals, and practices. At the apex of this diversity of religious culture, between the late tenth and the thirteenth centuries, the papal monarchy established a new legal standard for the recognition of sainthood—papal canonization.

The Peace Movement, Pilgrimage, and Crusade

Carolingian rule was a relatively brief experiment in a unified European Empire whose success was its unmaking. The local demand for a ruler of Carolingian blood during the ninth century fragmented the ruling dynasty, setting brother against brother and ushering in a period of political decentralization that generated violent competition for control of property and status among a mounted and armed class of local thugs whom in popular medieval imagery we recognize as knights. This arms-bearing elite specialized in castle-based extortion rackets, harrying peasant communities, and imposing on them new customs of rent and work disciplines that reduced them to servility.

In southern France, the atrocities (rape, torture, the burning of churches and villages, destruction of crops, looting, and kidnap) that miracle narratives of the time report as characterizing these developments might be safely regarded as exaggerated by bishops and abbots for the purpose of limiting, legitimizing, and controlling local political ambitions. This 'peace movement', which began around 975, and its later imposition of the 'Truce of God', from *c.*1030 onwards, proscribed violence on holy days, and imposed truces between warring lords and castellans at synods attended by monks accompanied by the bodies of saints. In June 989 the monks of Nouaillé journeyed to the council of Charroux, their relics of St Junianus performing miracles along the way. The bodies of the saints and reliquaries containing fragments of their remains were brought out in force from all over the neighbouring regions of Limousin and Poitou for the council. At meetings like these, relics were taken out and processed, and the powerful (*potentes*) were pressured by the bishops, monks, and the crowd into swearing peace oaths on them. The relics of St Stephen were used for this purpose at Bourges in 1038.

When saints failed to protect monastic property against malicious encroachment, monks might go on strike.

Liturgical devotion to a saint might be suspended for a period of ritual humiliation of the relics during which they were removed from a shrine and placed on the ground, sometimes surrounded by barricades of thorns. The shocking spectacle applied pressure on neutral witnesses who might seek a remedy to the stand-off between monks and encroachers. In England after the Norman Conquest the encroachment of new lords and agents of the king upon monastic estates is clear from accounts of saintly retaliations preserved by monks in newly commissioned miracle collections.

The more typical encounter between relics and lay people remained that of pilgrimage. Journeying to holy destinations (*ad loca sancta*) out of devotion to God fulfilled new roles in the later Middle Ages. Enshrined saints continued to serve the petitionary causes of local pilgrims suffering from ill health, injustice, or plain bad luck, but pilgrimage abroad might also be imposed by a parish priest or other confessor as penance for grave sin, or else prescribed in the rehabilitation of abjured heretics. The penitential motivation to pilgrimage in imitation of the wandering Irish monks of the seventh century and the apostles found other outlets in crusading, in the pursuit of religious indulgences, and in the birth of a whole new religious vocation, that of the mendicant orders, or friars, which from the thirteenth century produced some of the most famous saints of the middle ages.

The legitimizing role the church played in the feudal crisis of the tenth through the twelfth centuries found its greatest expression at the peace council of Clermont in November

1095, convened by Pope Urban II. Urban had been a grand prior of the abbey of Cluny, the most successful reform monastery of the age, which specialized in a combination of prayer for the dead, ceaseless and extravagant liturgy, and lavish hospitality irresistible to the new arms-bearing class, who gifted to Cluny huge endowments in order to be a neighbour of St Peter, the abbey's patron saint. We have no transcript of Urban's Clermont sermon, but accounts circulating in its wake associate it with the launching of a new lay religious vocation. Crusading combined armed pilgrimage to liberate Jerusalem and the Holy Land from the Infidel with the remission of punishment due to sin. It was a perfect solace and opportunity for Europe's knightly classes. St Bernard, the towering Cistercian monk of the twelfth century, wrote of the 'new knighthood' on behalf of an order of fighting monks, the Knights Templar. The Templars secured and protected travel routes for pilgrims to the Holy Land. Their counterparts, the Order of the Knights of St John, or Knights Hospitaller, provided lodgings and medical care in support of this new age of pilgrimage.

Monasteries back home benefited from the establishment of the crusader states in the East, receiving gifts of relics and other valuable materials from returning crusaders, and reviving the cults of their own enshrined saints to attract pilgrims along extensive routes across France, Spain, and Germany. The Galician cult of St James at Compostela became the premier destination for pilgrims in Europe, and could be reached via four distinct routes taking in among others, St Foy at Conques, the Virgin Mary at Le Puy and at Rocamadour, St Leonard de Noblat at his eponymous shrine, Mary

Figure 7 Statue of St Foy, *Maiestas*, Conques, France, ninth century.

Magdalene at Vézelay, and St Martin of Tours, along the Camino de Santiago (the way of St James). The skull of St Foy was encased by the ninth-century monks of Conques in a reliquary statue made of recycled pieces of antique silver (see Figure 7). It was taken out on feast-day processions, and a miracle collection survives testifying to the practice local women had of donating their jewellery, precious metal, and gems to the statue, some of which can be seen encrusting the metalwork.

Canterbury became one of the most important places on pilgrimage itineraries when, in 1170, knights of King Henry II's household murdered the incumbent archbishop, Thomas Becket. Becket's sanctity was immediately revealed in visions to lay folk who presently turned up at the scene of the martyrdom. His swift canonization in 1173 prepared the ground for St Thomas's translation in 1220, and for the production of stained-glass illustrations of miracles selected from several books of such stories compiled by monks at the cathedral.

Mendicant Saints

In imitation of the *vita apostolica*, new religious orders of the thirteenth century known as the mendicants or 'little brothers' (friars minor) grew from the efforts of two late medieval saints, Francis and Dominic. Of these two saints, it is perhaps Francis of Assisi who was to become the most famous of all late medieval saints. The son of an Italian cloth merchant, Francis famously renounced his family's great wealth to adopt the life of a hermit. One day at mass in the Church of St Mary the Angel in Assisi, he heard a reading from the

Gospel of Matthew (Chapter 10), calling the disciples to their vocation, 'Preach as you go, saying the kingdom of Heaven is at hand'. From that moment he went barefoot, pioneering a new kind of itinerant begging not seen since the earliest days of the Christian Church. In a moment of spiritual ecstasy he famously received an impression of the stigmata, the wounds of Christ, on his body.

The meaning of his life and legacy was bitterly contested. Official lives written by among others Thomas of Celano (in 1228, 1244–7, and 1254–7) and St Bonaventura (in 1260) reveal disputes, in their re-versioning of key events, among his followers and the church over how literally Francis intended his friars to imitate the life of the disciples. Factions formed. The Spirituals favoured absolute poverty and were excommunicated as heretics for rejecting a series of practical compromises (communal lodgings, books, and other material resources) considered necessary by the Conventuals for the support of the order's urban pastoral mission.

By contrast, St Dominic came from the Castilian aristocracy to be the founder of the Friars Preachers, a parallel experiment in apostolic living characterized by a greater intellectual and institutional focus than that of the Franciscans, reflecting Dominic's character and its formative role as a mission to the Albigensian heretics of southern France. Dominic's progressive organization of the order was adapted for use by the Franciscans. The Friars Preachers established branches in Bologna, Paris, and Oxford that they used to recruit talented young men to work in urban environments as preachers and confessors to the laity. The order furnished the Holy Inquisition with many of its personnel and two famous thirteenth-century doctors of the Church, St Thomas Aquinas and St Albert the Great, were Dominicans.

Papal Canonization

Until the late twelfth century, new saints were recognized locally under episcopal supervision. Beginning in 993 with the translation of St Ulric's relics by Liudolf, bishop of Augsburg, bishops had occasionally looked to Rome for papal confirmation of new saints. The first indication of an exclusive papal right of canonization appeared in a letter, known after its opening phrase *Audivimus* (Latin 'we hear'), of Pope Alexander III (1159–81) of 1171–2 to a Swedish king. The saint in question is unclear but the likeliest candidate, denounced by the letter as a drunkard, is King Erik of Sweden. The letter bluntly advises its recipient, a contestant to the throne and member of the family implicated in Erik's murder, 'even if prodigies and miracles were produced through his intermediary, you would not be permitted to venerate him publicly as a saint without the authority of the Roman Church'.

Around a dozen canonization procedures were lodged under Alexander III. In support of a claim, Popes conventionally began to require eyewitness accounts of miracles, the production of a *Vita*, and approval by a synod of bishops. Innocent III (1198–1216) called for evidence of moral virtue demonstrated by a life of honest conduct (*honestae conversationae*), death with a reputation for holiness (*fama sanctitatis*), and the virtue of signs (i.e. miracles) in death. 'That saints' relics may not be exhibited outside reliquaries, nor may newly discovered relics be venerated without authorization from the Roman Church' was established in canon sixty-two of the Fourth Lateran Council of 1215, over which he presided. His successor Pope Gregory IX made this canon law in his Decretals of 1234.

Papal canonization was not about making saints; sanctity was a God-given vocation. It confirmed the presence of the saint in eternal glory, instated the saint's feast day in the calendar of universal saints, and effectively regularized the public cult of a saint. Between 993 and 1500 there were seventy-eight papal canonizations, probably fewer than half the number of petitions actually initiated. It was an expensive business that could be frustrated by political machinations, whim, and historical contingency. One of those canonized in this period, St Thomas Aquinas (d.1274), was a theologian and Dominican friar canonized in 1323. Not known for heroic virtue or wonder-working powers (although stories of his absent-mindedness and youthful rejection of the sexual advances of a woman were used to flesh out the case), what undoubtedly won him canonization was his massive contribution to scholastic theology. His views on heroic virtue were to stress not the mastery through technical cultivation of character traits such as fortitude, prudence, justice, and temperance, as described in Aristotelian thinking, but the preparing and opening of oneself to divinely bestowed Christian virtues of faith, hope, and charity.

The sociological and geographical distribution of canonized saints across Christendom was uneven. This reflected a varied regional regard for papal authority, the wealth, inclination and procedural expertise of different administrative bodies, as well as the changing political and spiritual preferences of the papal *curia*. In the north-west of Europe, violent deaths and high status were the chief hallmarks of sanctity. In England, a disproportionately more frequent papal petitioner, bishops presented most canonization cases largely on behalf of their holy predecessors and monastic founders. In Mediterranean regions, ascetics and charismatics were prized over administrators or lawyers, and were hoisted to papal attention on groundswells of local, popular veneration as much as in the interests of exclusive institutions. The papacy might claim the monopoly of canonization, but they could not prevent canonization by traditional means. Throughout the later Middle Ages, bishops continued to initiate the majority of new cults locally, to commission books of miracles and liturgies, and to ignore the papal prohibition of new cults.

The stigmata St Francis received in an ecstatic moment of prayer was one very obvious visual illustration of Christo-mimetic spirituality. Figure 8 is another material cultural exploration of this theme. It is a micromosaic depicting the 'Man of Sorrows', a popular devotional subject of late medieval Europe. It was acquired by the Carthusians of Santa Croce in Gerusalemme, Rome, in about 1380, but was created by Orthodox Greek artists in *c.*1300. The surrounding elaborately compartmentalized panels, resembling a printer's letterpress tray, contain *autenticae*, or labels attached to relics, and so witnessing to a communion of saints in Christ. The particular 'Man of Sorrows' at the centre of this devotional switchboard acquired archetypal status as a likeness of the alleged true vision of Christ that Pope Gregory the Great

Figure 8 The 'Man of Sorrows' Greek Orthodox micromosaic, *c.*1300.

(d.604) received when he celebrated mass at the altar of that same church.

The Vernacularization of Cult

Saints, old and new, were woven into almost all aspects of religious and lay devotional life in later medieval Europe.

Saintly patronage in the early Middle Ages had tended to be controlled by monasteries, royalty, and aristocracy. However, from the thirteenth to the fifteenth centuries public orchestration of cults spread outwards to merchants, traders, craftsmen, and the people, in both urban spaces and their rural hinterlands. New forms of lay religious organization arose in addition to that provided by priests. The tertiary orders, the Beguines, lay confraternities and guilds, hospitals, and charitable foundations supporting the destitute, the condemned, and the dying, received new endowments and more socially diffuse, small-scale donations than the long-established monasteries. Saints became the patrons of new corporations and confraternities. They helped in the maintenance of civic religion by representing and protecting the city from outside forces, by providing its citizens with a common identity, a mechanism for reconciliation, and occasions for celebration and consolation through processions, plays, charitable operations, and in such everyday rituals as prayer and the lighting of candles.

In late twelfth-century Oxford, for example, St Frideswide became an important patron of the city's corporation, as Oxford's merchant oligarchy cemented their relationships through intermarriage and common devotion to the saint. In the fourteenth and fifteenth centuries the tanners of Norwich adopted as their patron little St William, the alleged twelfth-century victim of Jewish ritual murder, whilst London maidservants looked to their thirteenth-century Italian counterpart, St Zita, for help in finding lost keys. From the end of the thirteenth century, the peasant wine porters working between Cremona and Modena in northern Italy venerated one of their number, Albert of Villa D'Ogna, as a saint. None of these four saints was officially canonized until centuries later, yet their cults were a vibrant and powerful presence in people's daily lives.

The quotidian presence of saints would have been evident at the heart of parish-pump religion. Saints featured in annual feast days (often linked with market days), in church dedications, and were represented in the interior decorative fabric of churches as statues in rood lofts, in relief sculpture, in altars and their decorative linen covers, in wall paintings, and in stained glass. Common subjects treated in English parish church wall paintings were the Virgin and Child, St Michael and the Weighing of Souls (which sometimes featured a Virgin Mary tipping the scales), St Christopher carrying Christ on his shoulders, St Catherine, and St Margaret defeating the dragon.

Across half of Europe this was all about to change as a consequence of the sixteenth-century Reformation, the subject of Chapter 4.

4

Early Modern Sainthood

In the parish church of St Mary Magdalene, Crowmarsh Gifford, the north wall of the nave bears a simple memorial stone on which are inscribed the following words:

> An epitaph upon the death of Mistriss Bridgit Parsons, wife of Philip Parsons, Master of Arts, who chaunged earth for Heaven, September 29th 1645:
>
> Who reads the legends of the former ages, St Bridgets praise may find in sundrie pages,
>   Pope, poets, painters have both power and skill, to canonize, praise, paint what saints they will.
>   Such vaine helps doth not Bridgit Parsons need. Whose life and death proved her a saint in deed.
>   Then cease vaine teares make noe fruitles complaint. The earth hath lost, now heaven injoyes this saint.

It is not clear which of the two saintly Bridgets Magister Parsons refers to, the fifth-century Irish nun of Kildare, or the fourteenth-century noblewoman, mystic, and monastic founder, Bridget of Sweden. Clear from this touching inscription, however, is the contrast its author makes between the saint exalted in canon law, hagiography, and image, and the person all the more worthy of saintly regard for their life of simple piety.

In the same year as Bridgit Parsons' death, the Roman Church came to a decision on the matter of the sainthood of Pope Gregory X. The case for his canonization had been making its progress through the Congregation of Rites (the curial standing committee responsible for such matters in Rome) since 1622. What eventually did for him was the Congregation's failure to be convinced that the book of miracles at Gregory's tomb was a genuine medieval record of the saint's miraculous intercessions. It would be a further sixty-eight years for Gregory X to receive 'equipollent' canonization in universal recognition of his enduring local cult. What Gregory's case shows us is the greater stringency brought to canonization procedures in the generations after the Council of Trent (1563).

The contrasting meanings of sainthood reflected in these public utterances of 1645 reflect how far Christianity in Europe had diverged over the preceding century and a half. But these examples have ironies that betray the wrestling of both Catholic and Protestant churches with common questions of continuity and change. On one side is the English Protestant, Philip Parsons, condemning Catholics for vain poetic acts of cult promotion exactly as he publicly states his conviction in verse that his wife is a saint. And here is the Catholic Church in apostolic resplendence, confidently discarding medieval evidence for the sanctity of a papal predecessor. The canonization of Popes was never a formality, but the grounds on which Gregory's case foundered reveal the beginnings of a modernizing spirit in the post-Tridentine church. How had things come to this?

Continuity and Change

Criticism of the cult of saints existed prior to the Reformation. Guibert of Nogent had written a treatise on relic veneration in the early twelfth century berating neighbouring monasteries in his northern France for encouraging the veneration of spurious and impossible relics (including a tooth of Jesus Christ), for inventing cults to new saints on the flimsiest of evidence, and for doing all this for financial rather than spiritual gain. His work, *De Pignoribus Sanctorum*, was in part an assertion of the secondary importance of relics relative to the Eucharist, and a call for stricter pastoral supervision of cult activity, including the emphasis to be laid upon contrition over petition in the presence of relics.

From the thirteenth century to the fifteenth the church trimmed a more generous line in its attempts to temper religious enthusiasm for the cult of saints. Papal canonization procedures had instated an official sainthood, and church councils technically distinguished between acceptable and proscribed forms of religious practice, but these were hardly absorbed at the parish level. It was impossible to regulate the entirety of cult practice. Moreover, the church benefited from the entanglement of saints in a booming sacred economy centred on pilgrimage and the sale of indulgences. The relics of saints, including their bodily remains and contact items, effluvia such as dust, oil, and water, the Eucharist and sacramentals (objects blessed by priests), all exhibited miracle-working properties, as did the holy blood of Christ, and manifestations of stigmata (bleeding in imitation of Christ's wounds), reliquaries, and images.

The muddled coexistence of devotion and superstition continuously fed debate on the definition and significance of saints in the Christian faith. Renaissance humanism made an exciting contribution to such debates in its willingness to apply classical philosophical and literary concepts afresh to sacred texts. When it did so it drew attention to the weak scriptural footings underpinning medieval scholasticism, among them many of the assumptions underlying contemporary devotion to the saints. The most celebrated humanist scholar of his generation, the Augustinian canon Erasmus of Rotterdam, brought acute criticism cloaked in sardonic humour to clerical encouragement of popular religious practices. His *In Praise of Folly* is a satirical indictment of human foibles in the form of an encomium to the hitherto unacknowledged inspiration behind everyday acts of human idiocy: Foolishness. Behind the voice of an erudite fool, Erasmus criticized pilgrimage, the cult of saints, and the veneration of relics. What need—asked Folly—does Folly have of temples, 'why should I require incense, wafers, a goat or sow, when all men pay me that worship, everywhere which is so much approved even by our very divines [i.e. priests]?' When people light candles to the Virgin Mary in broad daylight, but fail to imitate her in 'pureness of life, humility, and love'; when statues and images are worshiped for saints; and coins accompany favours begged from saints, of 'what belongs to Folly'? Saints were not contractors offering specialist services for the price of a votive offering. The little rituals one observed at shrines were distractions from modern religious devotion (*devotio moderna*) based upon reflection on inward intention.

Erasmus lampooned the indulgence system that increasingly seemed to put religious devotion to the service of commercial interest. Through indulgences the church acted as 'creditor to the faithful' of the superabundant merit accrued by the Virgin Mary and the saints. The terms and conditions of such bestowals of merit, invaluable in reducing the time an individual might otherwise spend in purgatory, usually involved pilgrimage to a shrine, repeated participation in liturgical celebrations, the observance of contrition, prayerful invocation of saintly intercession, *and* a money offering. Though perhaps not the original intention, the fact that the indulgence was a transferable unit of merit quantifiable in monetary terms effectively made of sanctity an immensely popular commodity. Indulgences even took on some of the fungible qualities of money. Buyers of indulgences could forego religious observances by engaging a proxy pilgrim, and by the beginning of the sixteenth century the merit secured could be spent getting time off purgatory for dead relatives.

In 1515, Pope Leo X issued the bull *Sacrosanctis* granting an indulgence in order to leverage a bank loan that would see through to completion the protracted building work on St Peter's Basilica, Rome. The Pope's associate in the initiative, Albrecht, archbishop of Mainz, brought in Johann Tetzel, the talented Dominican inquisitor and preacher, to lead a marketing tour for the indulgence. The gratuitous nature of the campaign famously provoked the Augustinian friar,

Martin Luther, on 31 October 1517, to nail ninety-five theses refuting Tetzel's preaching to the door of the castle church in Wittenberg.

Saints and the Reformation

In German historical tradition, Luther's intervention inaugurated the Reformation, a struggle for the highest stakes between fierce adversaries over the relationship between church and state, the authority and mission of the Church, the fundamental doctrines of the Christian faith, and the conscience of every soul in Christendom. It spurred immense intellectual creativity, fuelled iconoclasm and bitter polemic, and brought protracted war and martyrdom. It ultimately divided Europe into the Catholic states of southern Europe and those states of northern Europe whose princes embraced various kinds of Protestantism.

The evangelical founders of the Reformation did not agree in all aspects of their theology, but common themes can be discerned. Men like Martin Luther, John Calvin, and Ulrich Zwingli argued for the wresting of religious authority away from priesthood and papacy, and the restoration of Jesus Christ and the word of scripture at the heart of Christianity. Luther became convinced by his reading of the Bible and Augustine that the prospect of salvation for sinful humans existed neither in good deeds nor the invocation of saints but entirely upon the grace God might bestow upon them.

The shifting focus of worship from the altar to the pulpit, and from the 'hocus pocus' of priestly ritual (a term believed to be a Protestant contraction of *hoc est corpus meum*, used to mock the Eucharistic sacrament) to justification 'by faith alone' (*sola fide*), had dramatic repercussions for the status of saints and for the relationships of the faithful with them. Saints were not abolished; their job description was revised in line with Luther's reading of justification by faith: 'inasmuch as the saints are always aware of their sin and seek righteousness from God in accord with his mercy, for this very reason they are also already regarded as righteous by God...they are actually sinners, but they are righteous by the imputation of a merciful God'.

The 'communion of saints' brought no abundance of merit. It comprised *all* who by faith alone might be cloaked by God in divine righteousness. A huge irrelevance was thus made of the Catholic Church's penitential system, of prayers for the dead, of the idea of good works and saintly intercession, of the cult of saints, the veneration of relics, and pilgrimage. That crystallization of Anglican doctrine, the Thirty-Nine Articles of 1563, had this to say on the subject: 'The Romish doctrine concerning Purgatory, Pardons, worshipping and adoration as well of Images as of Relics, and also Invocation of Saints, is a fond thing vainly invented, and grounded upon no warranty of Scripture; but rather repugnant to the word of God.'

A rip-off of Erasmus, Calvin's *Treatise on Relics* is a sweeping survey of relic-cults across Christendom detailing the disparate customs associated with Saints Peter and Paul, St Anne, St Mary Magdalene, St Denis, St Stephen, the Holy Innocents, Saints Gervase and Protase, St Sebastian, St Antony, and St Ursula and the 11,000 virgins, as well as

St John the Baptist, the Virgin Mary, and Christ. It ridicules the existence of multiple versions of the same relic (at least fourteen nails of the cross, scattered between Paris, Milan, Siena, Venice, and Rome; the coat of Jesus at Argenteuil *and* Trèves), and of items whose ancient provenance was barely credible (the holy blood of Christ surviving over several centuries in so many locations). Calvin exposed as a piece of pumice stone the brain of St John the Baptist and the arm of St Antony as a stag's bone, both prized possessions inspected at a shrine in Geneva. The number of fragments of the True Cross in weight resembled the cargo of a ship, hardly something a single human being could have carried on their back. A shoe belonging to John the Baptist had been stolen from the Carthusians of Paris, only to be replaced thanks to 'that sort of miracle never likely to cease so long as there are shoemakers in the world'. It all led for Calvin to the conclusion that 'The desire for relics is never without superstition and what is worse, it is usually the parent of idolatry'.

Iconoclasm

One solution to idolatry was iconoclasm, or the breaking of images, which could apply to the wholesale dismantling of all the material props of Catholic worship: wall paintings, stained glass, statues and shrines, altars and their crucifixes and richly decorative cloth coverings. The swift, brutal uprooting of all stimuli to idolatry was imposed by some Protestant authorities, independently executed by some more fanatical clerics and secular agents, and occasionally dramatically and spontaneously enacted by mobs of the disillusioned faithful. Despite the spontaneous violence and damage done in 1521–2 to the altars and images of Franciscan and Augustinian churches in Wittenberg, Lutheran church authorities were hesitant to carry through iconoclastic programmes. Luther did not go in for iconoclasm, which he felt just as indicative of religious misunderstanding as the ritualism of the Catholics. Lutheran churches continued to house statues and crucifixes, though they inhabited less prominent places in the church, on the understanding that such things could be appreciated without idolatry entering into it.

It was a different matter in those churches influenced by Calvin and Zwingli. From the 1520s to the 1540s, town councils in places like Zurich, Regensburg, Augsburg, Berne, and Basle commissioned the orderly removal of shrines and statues from churches, or else looked on at moments of popular vandalism of church property. Some images were placed in store, others removed by their donors, others destroyed; the saints depicted on rood screens and wall paintings might have their faces scratched out, glass be smashed. In a series of injunctions issued by Thomas Cromwell in 1538, wall paintings were covered over, the traditional rood loft statues of the Crucifixion flanked by Mary and St John were taken down, and the popular practice of offering candles before images banned. The Protestant Church in the Netherlands adopted a particularly austere and thorough policy of iconoclasm in the 1560s, statues being removed, and walls whitewashed.

The Reformation Martyrs

The joint enforcement of doctrinal uniformity and loyalty to the state by religious and secular authorities during the Reformation resulted in a new generation of martyr-saints plucked from communities who found themselves on the wrong side of confessional borders. Incidences of martyrdom fed into reform memories and polemic in different ways. Martyrs were particularly important to evangelical Protestants as a vindication of their sectarian claims to revealed religious truth. Luther saw contemporary martyrs as vivid, immediate evidence of God's living Word that granted true Christians an experience of conditions in the primitive church. He wrote hymns, letters, and responses to the early martyrs of German evangelicalism, Heinrich Vos and Johannes Esch, both executed in Brussels in 1523.

Protestant martyrologists took advantage of the first European age of print media to produce lavish written and visual memorials to their contemporary heroes. Jean Crespin, a French Protestant lawyer and publisher living in Geneva, compiled and published *Le Livre des Martyrs* in 1554. John Foxe's *Acts and Monuments* (1563), more commonly known as *Foxe's Book of Martyrs*, did for the history of Protestant England what Bede had done for the Anglo-Saxon Church. In imitation ultimately of Bede's martyrology, Foxe assembled a new configuration of martyrs from his and earlier ages, portraying in gruesome woodcuts English martyrs such as Ridley, Latimer, and Cranmer on their execution pyres, scrolls unfurling speech from their mouths as if from the pulpit. His book went through four editions within twenty-five years and became a canonical work of English hagiography, and a vaccine against Catholic infection to the English body politic.

English Catholics were obliged to be more discreet in the commemoration of their own recent martyrs. There was no question of them launching canonization procedures with Rome, however worthy of this their priests may have been. The young Jesuits who trained on the continent for service in Elizabethan England, many of whom ended up hanged, drawn, and quartered, seem unlikely descendants of those monk-missionaries Bede portrays in his *Ecclesiastical History of the English*. But recent scholarship suggests they did act with missionary intent rather than with limited pastoral aims. In their efforts to return the English people to the fold, they swathed their activities in an atmosphere of visions and miracles reminiscent of the early church. Moreover, there was an appetite among the people even in the later decades of Elizabeth's reign and into the early Stuart era for such providential signs and wonders, and for the relics of those who were martyred.

Whilst the medieval infrastructure of shrines was swept away by iconoclasm and, in England, the monasteries were dissolved, relics were salvaged and distributed privately among clandestine Catholic groups and recusant aristocratic families along with those of newly martyred Catholics. Stonyhurst College in Lancashire, originally a Jesuit foundation for exiled English Catholics of the late sixteenth century located on the continent (at Saint-Omer), possesses among its collection of martyr relics, the fourth-century body of

St Gordianus, and the ropes used to quarter St Edmund Campion.

As the new martyrs' relics went to ground, a sacred geography of places associated with Jesuit mission and ministry was discreetly and respectfully sustained in the pious memories of Catholic communities. Tyburn in London became a place of powerful religious spectacle and pilgrimage as the site where criminals and traitor-priests over several decades were executed. Among crowds that came out to see the heroic martyrdoms of Edmund Campion, Robert Southwell, and Thomas Maxfield, an anonymous few took splinters from the wooden gallows on which they were hanged, or else scattered flowers and herbs upon the ground on which they were drawn and quartered.

Catholicism drew upon its reserves of ancient martyrs, especially in the century and a half after the 'rediscovery' of the Roman catacombs in 1578, when thousands of ancient Roman human remains of unknown identity but popularly ascribed sanctity were exported north of the Alps to restock the relic collections of religious institutions and pious aristocratic families recently depleted by iconoclasm. The *Katakombenheiligen* (catacomb saints) of Burgrain, Roggenburg, Weyarn, and Kühbach are some of the most opulently dressed and materially enhanced bodily remains of saints one can imagine.

The Catholic Reformation and Saints

Despite spontaneous popular reverence cropping up around the Catholic martyrs of the Reformation, the Roman Catholic

Church canonized only two martyrs. Though it granted non-universal saintly status to fourteen men and women between 1523 and 1588, none received universal canonization in the same period. But the Protestant assault upon the cult of saints, the priesthood, and penitential system did not go unanswered.

The Council of Trent met for over twenty-five sessions between 1545 and 1563, and reasserted Catholic doctrine in a resounding response to Protestant heresy. The final session of the council, which took place on 3 and 4 December 1563, legislated 'On invocation, veneration, and the relics of saints, and on sacred images'. Bishops were to instruct the faithful that the veneration of saints 'reigning together with Christ', and the veneration of their relics in prayerful invocation carried blessings and merit; that 'images of Christ, the Virgin mother of God, and the other saints should be set up and kept...because the honour showed to them is referred to the original that they represent'; that sacred images were beneficial to the faithful who can 'thank God for them, shape their own lives and conduct in imitation of the saints, and be aroused to adore and love God and to practise devotion'; and finally that 'all superstition must be removed from invocation of the saints, veneration of relics, and use of sacred images, all aiming at base profit must be eliminated, all sensual appeal must be avoided so that images are not painted or adorned with seductive charm'. Various anathemas accompanied these doctrinal statements that were directed against reform statements rejecting the cult of saints as superstition.

Another important facet of the renewed Catholic Church was the organization of the annual cycle of liturgical offices. The Council of Trent mandated the introduction of an official Roman Breviary (a calendrically arranged collection of hymns, prayers, biblical readings, psalms, hagiography, and orders of service) that for the first time established a uniform liturgical programme throughout the Church. Some saints' days were removed from the calendar to address the late medieval imbalance between festal (saints) and ferial (regular) days. In addition, there were also loopholes that allowed for local custom. Religious orders were allowed to retain their own breviaries, and local bishoprics and archbishoprics that could demonstrate their breviaries were older than two hundred years were also allowed to keep their liturgical customs.

A third reform to canonization procedure was begun by the Council of Trent and continued until 1642. In that year legislation introduced since 1588 was codified in a comprehensive decretal. The essential structure of the medieval canonization process remained in place. There were four stages: the local bishop would gather evidence to make the case for the canonization of a particular candidate for sainthood (*processus ordinarius*); once submitted, this triggered another local inquiry, but this time under the direct authority of Rome, into the quality and veracity of the evidence. This involved the fuller interrogation of local witnesses according to headings approved by Rome (*processus apostolicus*). These materials were then sent to the Congregation of Rites where they were examined by a figure popularly known as the devil's advocate who raised written objections to what he regarded as problematic claims. These were then answered, as best as they could be, by a person deputed by those who were supporting the candidate. All this by now voluminous material was read by three cardinals and summarized in the form of a biography of the candidate, statement of their virtues illustrated with examples, and finally a collection of miracles. After reading the summary account, the Pope then ruled on the matter.

Adjustments to this system over the period up to 1642 reveal an interesting dance between powerful local interest groups within the church, and that coalition of disparate groups that collectively constituted the great edifice of papal authority. Powerful individuals often had a foot in both camps. Whilst successive rulings tended to impart a centralizing impetus to procedures, they reveal the efforts of the papacy to make accommodations with local innovators.

The enthusiasm with which some holy men and women were venerated often led technically to communities jumping the gun with their veneration of an un-canonized saintly candidate. In many ways this was a continuation of the medieval habits the Tridentine Church sought to end. A holding category of holy person, the 'new blesseds' (*beati moderni*), emerged in this period, to describe the objects of a local cult yet to receive papal confirmation as saints, but who received official acknowledgement through beatification. Further regulation came in the 1620s. A ruling in 1624 required a fallow period of ten years be imposed between the processes *ordinarius* and *apostolicus*. The Congregation of the Holy Office in 1625 banned the placement of candles and votive offerings before images or statues of holy persons not yet canonized, and in the following year a fifty-year delay was placed on the public discussion of new cults.

The first newly canonized saint for sixty-five years was announced in 1588 by Sixtus V. St Diego of Alcalá was a fifteenth-century Spanish Franciscan. St Hyacinth, the early thirteenth-century Polish Dominican, was the next to be canonized in 1594. Between 1588 and 1767 there were fifty-five canonizations, two in the sixteenth century, twenty-four in the seventeenth, and twenty-nine in the eighteenth. Up to the year 1665 there had been only four-teen (among whom were three women, five founders of religious orders, and twelve from either Italy or Spain). The majority of Tridentine saints were male and belonged to religious orders or the new religious societies such as the Jesuits, or else were secular clergy. They were often Italian and Spanish aristocrats. There were no theologians and the only two martyrs living in Europe were Jan of Nepomuk (d.1393 and can.1729), and Fidelis of Sigmaringen (d.1622 and can.1746).

Hundreds of local holy persons who died *in fama sanctita-tis* (with saintly reputation) were never put forward for canonization. Others, like Gregory X, had their status pend-ing for several decades, and up to 1665, twenty-seven candidates never made it beyond beatification. The existing Congregation of the Holy Office (the official name for the Inquisition) continued to be involved in investigating local cults for irregularities, but was joined in the administration of canonization procedures by the newly constituted Congre-gation of Rites and Ceremonies. Both these bodies provided a buffer between the Church and potential unorthodoxy, and a holding operation on the impresarial ambitions of bishops and local churchmen. Powerful churchmen with links to Rome and a local ecclesiastical base could quite successfully circumvent these obstacles, especially if, like Cardinal Borromeo, archbishop of Milan, they were champions of Counter-Reformation values. Not since the days of St Ambrose himself had the Milanese seen a bishop so devoted to the incorporation of the cult of saints into his pastoral strategy for the city and archdiocese.

The Reformation witnessed a change in the image of the Christian saint. Protestant churches revived a notion of the community of saints that would have been familiar to contemporaries of St Paul, although with the addition among the godly elect or visible saints of Europe and the Anglophone colonies of North America of various sectarian distinctions to their experiments with communal morality. A new emphasis in the Catholic Church on moral character over signs and wonders made for a particular kind of Counter-Reformation saint who could be dynamic and cosmopolitan in an age of colonial expansion to the New World and the Far East. These figures are described in the remaining chapters.

5

Gendering the Saints

Historically, men have always received greater public recognition for their sanctity than women. The *Synaxarion of Constantinople*, a calendar of saints' days compiled in early eleventh-century Byzantium, lists fifty-five female martyrs up to the fourth century, eighteen holy-women from the fourth to the sixth century, none in the seventh, and eight in the eighth and ninth. The tenth century saw five biographies of women saints. Women fared almost as badly in the Latin West. The low point was in the eleventh and twelfth centuries, when women accounted for a little over ten per cent of new saints. Twenty-five per cent of canonizations from the thirteenth to the fifteenth century were of women. Thereafter, up to the seventeenth century, the proportion of female canonizations fluctuated around fifteen per cent. Four women were canonized between 1198 and 1431: St Catherine of Siena, St Bridget of Sweden, St Elizabeth of Hungary, and St Hedwig of Silesia.

In Spite of Their Sex

Why were women so consistently under-represented among those venerated as saints? The church is historically a patriarchal institution (think of the nomenclature of its leaders, 'abbot' (father), 'Pope' (papa), and 'patriarch' (tribal father)) even as it styles itself the 'mother church'. An abiding sense that sainthood is a male distinction, that women are religious in spite of their sex, that asceticism and spirituality are naturally more difficult for women, and perhaps of secondary importance when practised by them, is part of its patriarchal outlook. Clare of Assisi's male hagiographer depicted her not as imitating Christ but as imitating Christ's imitator, St Francis, even though we know directly from Clare's own writings that *imitatio Christi* fired her spiritual imagination. These views meshed with other historically patriarchal discourses, for example, that of the family, and of medical and philosophical knowledge.

Pope John Paul II's apostolic letter of 1994, *Ordinatio Sacerdotalis*, clarified that the Church's lack of authority to ordain them did not indicate the 'lesser dignity' of women. Still, it is difficult to see what comfort women might take from being barred from ministering as priests, a conventional attribute of confessor-saints, and having the Blessed Virgin Mary held up as proof that the church honours female religious vocations. The road to sanctity for women has always been narrower and steeper than that for men. But, this chapter will show, not impassable.

An optimistic (and realistic) insight of women's history is that patriarchies of all sorts abide but human beings do not always dance to their tune. Those aspects of inherited knowledge, institutional rules, and customary habit that lent a 'natural' legitimacy to social roles based on sexual difference might always change in the everyday interactions of men and women, and sometimes even mutate under certain conditions. To illuminate the kind of statistics we saw at the beginning of this chapter we shall need to understand the contexts in which different varieties of female sanctity emerged and flourished in the past.

Bodies, the Life Cycle, Gender, and Sainthood

Christian understandings of bodily health and sexual difference were grounded in the Hippocratic system of humoralism championed in the second century CE by the great medical philosopher Galen. According to this system, the female body was naturally disadvantaged in its humoral composition; whilst men were hot and dry by temperament, women tended to an excess of wetness and cold that necessitated the monthly expulsion of surplus, non-combusted matter. Galenic theory clearly privileged the male over the female form, and Christianity absorbed and placed a further moral gloss on this conventional medical knowledge. Male asceticism offered a moral standard of self-discipline that kept at bay the effeminizing influences of over-indulgence in rich food and sexual transgression (whether masturbation or fornication). As heiresses to the sin of Eve, women were thought to suffer pain in childbirth and to be naturally sinful (vain, wanton, quarrelsome, and inconstant)—difficult prejudices to overcome in the hope of saintly recognition.

The social implications of this dichotomy were clear. Late Roman Christianity assigned active roles to men and a passive role to women in its treatment of the life cycle of the body. Men perfected their character through moderation and self-control as the *paterfamilias* in their household and in that wider realm of public affairs, the *res publica*. Ascetic practice mapped out a higher road to sainthood for generations of monks and hermits. By contrast, for a young woman the prospect before her was early marriage to a much older man and a long, attritional slog through repeated cycles of pregnancy and childbirth before premature death, remarriage or, if lucky, survival into widowhood. This life cycle was remarkably consistent for most women throughout the pre-industrial age.

But there was some good news. The gradient between men and women was softened by Augustine's caution that asceticism could incubate one of the worst kinds of sin, spiritual pride. Secondly, if women were physically inferior, their souls were of equal status to those of men. Aside from the opportunities this gave women to transcend their sexual frailties, these two facts provided monks with useful literary material to instruct their novices. Stories of transvestite saints, women whose asceticism was so convincingly manly that it allowed them to pass their lives as monks without suspicion, in part appear to fulfil this function. St Marina, for example, out of filial piety, cut her hair and followed her father into a monastery (in the Kadisha Valley of sixth-century Syria). Marina was shunned from the monastery and reduced to begging at its gates under scandalous accusations of having fathered a child with the daughter of a local publican. The physical impossibility of her having committed such a sin was revealed only after her death, the narrative barb for those monks who likely comprised its primary audience being her extraordinary humility and charity (implicitly calling into question their own) in sleeping rough and nurturing the child foisted on her by the landlord.

Brides of Christ

Marina's loyalty towards her father is an unusual theme in the stories of early Christian female saints among whom spiritual awakening conventionally occasioned disobedience to the father or abandonment of duties towards family. Among that group of apocryphal acts, gospels and revelations of early Christian literature is the *Acts of Paul and Thecla*. Thecla was a disciple of St Paul granted apostolic licence by him to travel and preach. In the course of her virgin life Thecla faced down two attempts to have her murdered, evaded detection dressed as a man, and baptized herself. At its end, Thecla escaped the debauched intentions of a gang of devil-driven young men, when, under siege at her cave hermitage, a rock opened up to receive her. The absence of a body did not deter fifth-century Christians from commemorating the place of her 'assumption' at Meriamlik, Seleucia, and compiling an extensive collection of her miracles there.

Whether or not Thecla existed, her fanciful story was popular among early Christian audiences. Such literature enabled communities to graft imaginative offshoots onto biblical stories that rehearsed tensions and fantasies through themes of conflicted loyalties and religious vocation that were presumably topical to their readership. We have already heard the story of Perpetua, nursing mother and pious daughter, who gave up her baby child and disobeyed her father to meet martyrdom in the service of a higher authority. Another contemporary work, the *Acts of Peter*, famous for relating that St Peter was crucified upside down, describes him persuading a wife to leave her husband to follow her faith. The drama and the romance of these immensely rich stories in part muse on the challenge of Matthew 10:37: 'Anyone who loves their father or mother more than me is not worthy of me; anyone who loves their son or daughter more than me is not worthy of me.' In Thecla's story arises the same conflict between a mother, Theocleia, and her daughter, whose life is transformed after hearing St Paul preach and abandoning her fiancé to follow him. Apart from revealing an open mind among at least some second-century Christians about women as wandering, preaching apostles, Thecla's story set a narrative pattern revisited in subsequent hagiography, and which inspired countless young women, indirectly or otherwise, as we see in the sixth-century *Passion of Eugenia*, where the heroine, the daughter of an Egyptian Roman official, reads the *Acts of Paul and Thecla* and converts to the religious life, entering a monastery dressed as a man.

Virginity

Thecla is mentioned in a famous letter written by Jerome to the fourth-century virgin bride of Christ, Eustochium. Eustochium was the youngest of three daughters of the wealthy and pious widow, Paula, who took on Jerome after the death of his patron, Pope Damasus, in 384. Having perhaps closely observed his old patron's methods (Damasus's nickname was *auriscalpius matronarum* 'tickler of ladies' ears'), Jerome began correspondence with a collection of nubile Roman women more accustomed to the discreetly salacious, Tatleresque attention of the society marriage-market than the spiritually intimate and erotic imagery of the *Song of Songs*. But this is what he served them up in a mischievous mix of biblical citation, social satire, and devious charm. 'My object is not' he disingenuously writes in one letter, 'to praise the virginity which you follow, and of which you have proved the value, or yet to recount the drawbacks of marriage, such as pregnancy, the crying of infants, the torture caused by a rival, the cares of household management'. Jerome's letters became models of spiritual grooming much imitated by succeeding centuries of avowed male religious seeking to offer women instruction, encouragement, and protection in exchange for material and spiritual patronage.

Divinely-assisted flight from sexual labour, whether onward to an early martyrdom or to become a bride of Christ, is a theme in medieval stories of virgin princesses. St Aethelthryth was an East Anglian princess of the seventh century who preserved her virginity through two marriages, persuading her first husband to respect her religious vocation, and fleeing the second, King Ecgfrith of Northumbria, to found monasteries in Ely, East Anglia. St Frideswide, the eighth-century daughter of a Mercian sub-king, successfully resisted the rapacious advances of a royal suitor by releasing him from divinely-imposed blinding. This twelfth-century story is put to a familiar use in holding the Augustinian canons among whom she dwelt in her Oxford shrine to their mettle: 'Oh, unhappy men of today whose God is their belly, who glory in shame . . . all marvelled to see the frail sex at so young an age surpassing masculine strength.'

Widows

In one of his famous letters, Jerome rather ungallantly depicted widows as hypocrites who, 'seeing that priests cannot do without them, are lifted up into pride; and as, having had experience of both, they prefer the licence of widowhood to the restraints of marriage, they call themselves chaste livers and nuns. After an immoderate supper, they retire to rest to dream of the apostles'. The caricature reveals a fundamental ambivalence churchmen shared at the 'licence' widowhood gave powerful women such as Paula and St Fabiola (whose romantic portrait appears on the cover of this book), another immensely wealthy Roman patron of Jerome, as dowagers of independent means, as diplomatic 'hinges' between important families, as the influential mothers of important men and, in the case of royal families, as empresses and queen-regents; in short, at the power it gave women to command their respect.

That more than half the Byzantine women saints of 700–1450 were widows demonstrates the serious attention churchmen paid these women. In the early Medieval West, powerful lone women—like St Aethelthryth, St Radegund of Poitiers, and Queen Balthild in the sixth and seventh centuries, and St Adelaide and St Matilda in the tenth—were similarly feted. They founded monasteries, and became abbesses, or adopted a spiritual life of prayer and charity that won them public veneration. Just like Marcella and Paula in Jerome's Rome, they consulted with and gently directed holy-men, swapped relics with bishops, abbots, and lay rulers, influenced episcopal appointments, and endowed monasteries with the will and the means to commemorate them as saints.

We must not over-emphasize the progressive dimension to all this, or be tempted to associate the sanctity of these high-status female saints with some essential notion of female, let alone feminist, morality. For these complex and powerful women, however, who were perfectly capable of recognizing the flattery of churchmen and their precarious dependence on male kin, sanctity was always a political craft as well as a personal vocation.

The High Middle Ages

The thirteenth century was a high point for female sanctity in the Medieval West. Among those women recognized as saints were the princesses of Central European kingdoms, including Elizabeth of Hungary, Margaret of Hungary, Agnes of Bohemia, and Anne of Poland. Their lives reflect a familiar path negotiated between kin and church, and combined a royal mystique with the asceticism of the Cistercians and the apostolic poverty of the mendicant orders. Elizabeth of Hungary is distinguished as one of the few contemporary saints to appear in the *Golden Legend* of Jacobus de Voragine (d.1298). Elizabeth died aged twenty-four in 1231 and was canonized in 1235. After entering into marriage in obedience to her father, King Andrew II of Hungary, Elizabeth survived her husband, Louis IV, Landgrave of Thuringia, arranged for the alternative care of her three children, and followed the holy vocation of a devout lay widow, serving in a hospital at Marburg under Franciscan spiritual supervision.

Beguines, Mystics, and Heretics

From the thirteenth to the eighteenth centuries, the urban Low Countries and cities in northern Germany were the setting for communities of laywomen who mixed pious and active lives in the community with an enclosed and contemplative spiritual vocation. Male interpreters and confessors, in the form of friars or parish priests, who not only esteemed but knew how invaluable they were to urban religious and civic life, provided useful advocacy and protection to such women, and often ended up writing their Lives. The twelfth-century bishop and preacher, Jacques de Vitry, supported the Beguines in Liège and wrote a Life of Marie D'Oignies, a Flemish Beguine from Nivelles.

But other churchmen saw the Beguines and women mystics as a threat. Gilbert of Tournai (d.1284), master of Paris University and a Franciscan, described them as *mulierculas* (little women), and in his sermon on St Catherine of Alexandria—to the Beguines an inspirational teacher and preacher of the early church—made sure to depict her as obedient to the Church and talented only by uniquely divine assistance. Marguerite Porete, a highly-educated French Beguine, wrote *The Mirror of Simple Souls*, a work of Old French exploring the nature of the mystical union between

God and the human soul. The book was deemed heretical, however, and in 1310 Marguerite was burned at the stake in Paris. The Council of Vienne (1311–12) suppressed the béguinages over concerns that they were leading the laity astray with false teaching about the Trinity and the Holy Spirit. But the Beguines had a powerful supporter in Count Robert de Béthune of Flanders, who petitioned Pope John XXII to have their distinctive grey habits restored to them and their lives as 'good women who serve God' recognized. He particularly prized their civic role as moral educators of the young women of local town worthies.

Around many of these women, understood to have strayed too far from orthodoxy in their ecstatic behaviour, inward-turning and sometimes emotionally-raw spirituality, loomed accusations of demonic possession and the danger of heresy charges. Joan of Arc is perhaps the most famous example of a woman mystic found guilty of heresy and burned at the stake, though admittedly her indictments (including one of 'obdurate cross dressing') and conviction were clearly politically-motivated. She was only canonized in 1920. Let us now consider three portraits of female sanctity, women who shared a name but found their own distinctive paths to sainthood.

Teresa of Ávila

A towering figure of female sanctity, meditative and active, orthodox and ecstatic, emerged from a religious movement of late fifteenth-century Spain. The *beatas*, or blessed women, were an important lay presence among the *alumbrados* (enlightened ones), an eventually suppressed reforming movement within the peninsular which drew, dangerously from their rivals' perspectives, on the spiritual traditions of Andalusian Islam and Judaism. A just acceptable iteration of this movement was the Order of Discalced Carmelites of Ávila, founded by Teresa of Ávila (d.1582). The reforming Spanish nun wrote several books at the request of her confessors and Jesuit and Franciscan acquaintances, including an autobiography, a spiritual guide, *The Way of Perfection*, for the nuns of St Joseph's, her foundation of barefoot Carmelites in Ávila, and her masterpiece of Christian mysticism, *The Interior Castle*. Her autobiography guided countless women readers in prayerful ascent to a state of rapture, which 'is, as a rule, irresistible. Before you can be warned by a thought or help yourself in any way, it comes as a quick and violent shock'. Teresa was canonized in 1622, her autobiography seen as a classic of Spanish literature, her status as national patron saint rivaling that of Santiago himself.

Teresa was a trouble-causer, a shaker and a stirrer of the religious order to which her father sent her, and even as her strict but practical and unpretentious brand of reform combined an active and contemplative role for her nuns that was ambitious for its times, she proved too useful a bolster of Counter Reformation morale to attract ultimate censure. From a wealthy *converso* family (i.e. with mixed Jewish Christian heritage), Teresa breathed a new moral life into Carmelite spirituality that appealed to the affluent Spanish families who provided the resources and the recruits for her breakaway urban foundations of nuns. Religious men would find themselves uncomfortably attracted by the homeliness, affection, and humility of her correspondence, and in awe of her spiritual conviction and reforming energy. There is a hint of the Iron Lady, Margaret Thatcher, in her ability to motivate talented men around her. One of these talented younger disciples was John of the Cross, a Carmelite who helped her extend spiritual reform into new male foundations of religious, who protected her legacy against reactionaries within the Order, and who would himself be canonized in 1726.

Thérèse of Lisieux

Thérèse of Lisieux died of tuberculosis in 1897 at the age of twenty-four, having been a nun at the Carmelite convent of Lisieux for nine years. Within twenty-eight years Thérèse had been canonized. Since then, her cult has grown exponentially in her native France and throughout the world. Her story is remarkable for its re-envisioning of all the familiar tropes of heroic virtue, and for the interpretive control her three sisters, Marie, Pauline, and Céline—who were also nuns at the Carmel of Lisieux—insisted on exercising over her posthumous cult. It would be a mistake to see her cult as symptomatic of religious sentimentalism, or to scoff at its childish and feminine appeal. Behind Thérèse's profession of simple faith, humility, and childlike confidence in God's forgiveness and love, and in her embrace of 'the little way' and devotion to the holy face of Jesus, existed a steely and sober ambition to imitate the lives of the saints in her own way. As a result, not only novice nuns under her tuition but priests sought her out for spiritual guidance, and she was unafraid to give it to them.

If her sisters could not emulate Thérèse's sanctity in life, then the holy chutzpah they employed in the management of her posthumous image and spiritual message shows they were certainly chips off the same block (for more of which see Chapter 9). Thérèse's sister Pauline supervised and heavily revised the saint's spiritual writings, and Céline restricted access for commercial purposes only to those photographic images approved of and often retouched by her (see Figure 9), in a remarkable early example of modern mass-media branding. By these means was the Catholic Church beguiled into the speedy canonization of a saint immensely popular among ordinary women and men.

Figure 9 Photograph of St Thérèse of Lisieux.

Mother Teresa

The current director of the Vatican's Press Office, Fr Federico Lombardi, recently divulged a personal anecdote of Pope Francis meeting the Albanian nun, Agnes Gonxha Bojaxhiu, at an episcopal synod in 1994, and finding her 'a strong woman, a woman able to give courageous testimony...I would have been afraid to have had her as my superior, since she was so tough'. Mother Teresa of Calcutta (d. 1997) was in many people's eyes a living saint. Her foundation of the Missionaries of Charity in 1950, and work among the gravely ill and poorest of the world, won her a holy reputation that has provoked contrasting views. To some, Teresa gave profound testimony to the simplest of Christian premises, 'blessed are the meek (or poor) for they shall inherit the earth' (Matthew 5.5). Critics, however, pointed to reports of outmoded, unhygienic medical practices in her clinics, lack of palliative care, and, perhaps less surprising, rejection of contraception, as betraying a fixation with the aestheticization of poverty and suffering over its eradication. What cannot be denied is the love and toil that Teresa put into alleviating the stigma attached to those of extreme poverty and unacknowledged suffering. Having recently approved a second attribution of miraculous intercession to her, Pope Francis will soon get the chance to canonize this tough woman who, he admits, intimidated him just a little bit when he met her aged eighty-four.

We should expect nothing less of a female saint.

6

The Blessed Virgin Mary

The Blessed Virgin Mary is pre-eminent among Christian saints. Her giving birth to Jesus the God-man distinguishes her from other women, even as it draws attention to that experience uniquely distinguishing women from men: childbirth. This delicate partitioning of empathetic possibilities in the veneration of Mary, intimately grounded in biology and played out through ideas of gender difference, has stimulated profound and sometimes conflicted religious emotions in men and women. St Mary presents a conundrum to Christian theology. A mother who remained a virgin, a Jew who became a Christian, a redeemer of humanity from the sins of Eve, a human who gave birth to God, and the Queen of Heaven; the Vatican has an army of Marian scholars, such is her implication in Christology, ecclesiology, hagiology, and in understandings of the theology of redemption, salvation, and intercession. It is perhaps surprising then to discover how little Mary features in the Gospels.

Perhaps the most troublesome issue for the early Christian Church was the nature of the Incarnation, and related to it, inevitably, the role and status of Jesus's mother. The doctrine of Mary as *Theotokos* (the God-bearer) grew in the fourth century and was fixed in Orthodox tradition at the Council of Ephesus in 431. The fifth-century Bishop Nestorius of Constantinople rejected the perilously vaulting honour the concept bestowed upon Mary, and its unbalanced rendering of the Incarnation. Surely Mary the *Christotokos* (bearer of the anointed one), in recognition of the human aspect of Jesus Christ, was more accurate?

In the Roman Catholic tradition, Mary became 'Mother of Christ' and, according to Bishop Ambrose of Milan, of the entire Christian Church. Mary was a ubiquitous figure of medieval veneration, celebrated and recreated in music, in sacred and pictorial arts, in book illumination, and in architecture and stained glass. Craftsmen depicted the Blessed Virgin Mary in frescoes, painting, sculpture, woodwork, and metalwork according to iconographical conventions dictated by ecclesiastical and lay patrons in a thousand different local settings. The doctrine of Mary's bodily Assumption into Heaven led churches to claim possession of her garments or milk as relics. A series of feast days developed in different liturgical traditions commemorating her Purification, the Assumption, the Nativity, the Annunciation, the Visitation, and, precociously championed by the monks of eleventh-century England, the Immaculate Conception. The Immaculate Conception, the doctrine of Mary's conception without stain of sin, was too controversial to become universally observed, at least until the nineteenth century when Pope Pius IX issued the bull, *Ineffabilis Deus*, establishing its canonical authority.

The twelfth century saw the collection by Anglo-Norman monks of Marian legends featuring Mary's especial power as an intercessor of final resort for those in sinful despair or extreme peril. A favourite among these is the story of Theophilus, a medieval Faustus figure, who signs a contract with Satan renouncing God for worldly preferment. His only hope was ultimately to call upon the Virgin Mary for help in dissolving the contract and restoring some grace in him before the sight of God. For all those with a heavy conscience afraid to meet their maker without good warrant from a personal advocate, Mary was repeatedly shown in these stories stepping up where other saints feared to tread.

In these early exemplary collections, a genre that expanded and diversified in the thirteenth century, was revived an old theme of Mary as scourge of the Jews. Versions of the Theophilus story have him introduced to Satan by Jewish sorcerers. In the same religious milieu emerged the first case in Europe of the blood libel accusation levelled at the Jews of Norwich. When the remains of a young boy called William were found in a wood outside the city, the monks of the cathedral priory accepted them as the relics of a martyr, and with some success promoted the cult of little St William of Norwich. The architectural programmes and exempla produced at the Gothic cathedral of Chartres, a church dedicated to the Virgin Mary, shared in these pullulating stories of encounter between Jewish maleficence and Marian justice.

In its return to the scriptures, and general draining of holiness away from its medieval conduits of shrine, relic, image, and altar, Protestantism reduced the liturgical, intercessory, and popular devotionally derived responsibilities the perceived abundance of her grace placed upon Mary.

Instead it assigned her mundane duties in the holy family as an exemplar of pious female domesticity, in Luther's words, 'milking the cows, cooking the meals, washing pots and kettles, sweeping out the rooms'. In fact, Mary's domestication within the extended holy family had already begun in fifteenth-century Europe with her regular depiction accompanied by St Anne, her mother, and St Elizabeth, mother of John the Baptist, a move perhaps intended to counter her own heavenward-spiralling majesty.

In Renaissance paintings, Mary often appears as a young woman, her intercessory power underlined by the numerous depictions of her introducing one saint or another to her child. Here is St Catherine beckoned by the Virgin to receive a spousal ring from the Christ child, here is St George in full armour, or St Antony in desert garb, all granted audiences by the Virgin. The Holy House of Walsingham, a staged pilgrimage setting of the childhood home of Christ at the Norfolk priory famously mocked by Erasmus, restored a similar accessibility to Mary. The theme of Mary as teacher flourished from the twelfth century, opening her son Jesus's heart to the teachings of the Lord, making of her a model of the mother as a source of moral instruction.

Militant Mary

The late medieval wars of conquest fought by knights and princes of northern Spain's Christian kingdoms against Muslim rulers in the Iberian Peninsula, romantically known as the *Reconquista*, found new roles for Mary. Mary accompanied Christian armies into the battlefield in her image on royal banners, and by their invocation of her in the battle cries, visions, and singing of the *Salve Regina*. Chronicle accounts of her interventions fed martial ambition with a sense of righteous destiny in this frontier warzone. King Alfonso VIII of Castile (d.1214) plunged into the enemy with a royal banner carrying her image at the decisive battle of Las Navas de Tolosa (1212). James I of Aragon (d.1276) wove his devotion to Mary into a biographical account of his martial deeds, describing how, having won safe passage to the island after praying to Mary, *maris stella* (Star of the Sea), his men charged against the Saracens at the siege of Majorca yelling 'Saint Mary'. Alfonso X (d.1284) supervised the collection of over four hundred popular songs known as the *Cantigas de Santa Maria*, allegedly writing some of them himself.

Mary's miraculous deeds burgeoned in the chronicles and in the hearts of kings happy to see dynastic legend wrapped in the divine vindication of the Queen of Heaven, and in those of knights hungry for land, plunder, justification, and succour through those horrible extremes of libidinous, violent action that fashioned them as honourable and powerful men. Mary was, according to Amy Remensnyder, their 'merciful mother, lady love, and virgin warrior' companion.

Behind the relationships knights forged with the Virgin on the battlefield lay more exquisite associations cultivated by the religious men who wrote the chronicles and fed the spiritual imagination of the age. The Cistercians, whose churches were all dedicated to the Virgin, adored Mary as their special patron. Homilies and sermons, commentaries and treatises explored all aspects of her role in the unfolding of salvation, in her relationship to the Trinity, her powers as a Redeemer, and her example to monks as the Virgin open to God. In a sermon prepared for the Assumption, St Ailred of Rievaulx instructed his monks to look to the Virgin Mary as a tower of faith, and her body as home to the Trinity. His work, *Jesus at the Age of Twelve*, showed monks how to reflect on the intimate relationship between mother and child and to immerse themselves in its spiritual possibilities. In style it imitates the commentaries and sermons of St Bernard of Clairvaux on the *Song of Songs*, whose poetic and erotic language stimulated Marian devotion. A story survives illustrating his particular devotion to Mary in which, while praying at her statue in the cathedral of Speyer, the Virgin Mary nourished him with milk sprayed from her bosom. In the Coptic Church, the image of Mary suckling her baby has deep cultural resonances for the faithful, resembling that of Isis, the Egyptian goddess of fertility typically depicted breastfeeding her son Horus. The vulnerability of those ancient Egyptian rural communities to periodic famine elevated Isis in their devotions, and Mary's role as protector and mother of all (*Mater Omnium*) succeeded Isis in them.

Modern Mariophanies

In the modern era reports of Marian apparitions have increased in times and places undergoing social stress, whether it be the disruption of working communities by industrial development and rapid cultural change, or strife caused by communal and civil conflict. In 1830, Catherine Labouré saw an apparition of the Virgin crowned with stars that was commemorated in the production of a 'Miraculous Medal'. The Virgin appeared several times to a poor village girl, Bernadette Soubirous, in 1858, in the remote Pyrenean town of Lourdes, declaring herself 'the Immaculate Conception'. Mary appeared in 1876 to five girls in the woods of Marpingen, Germany, again announcing herself as the Immaculate Conception. In 1917, the Virgin appeared to three shepherd children of Fatima, Portugal, with three prophecies and a general message of penitence involving daily use of the rosary and acts of reparation for sinners. In 1968, the Virgin Mary appeared on the roof of the Coptic Church of the Virgin Mary in Zeitoun, Cairo. In Champion, Wisconsin (1859), Pontmain, France (1871), Knock, Ireland (1879), Medjugorje, Bosnia-Herzegovina (1981), Kibeho, Rwanda (1981), and more recently in Alqosh, Northern Iraq (2015), the Virgin has appeared, most often to children, and with a warning of end-times and the need for repentance. Mary's increasing epiphanic importance to the faithful speaks to a diffuse and profound emotional space people have in their hearts, at times of extreme stress, for a female protector and creator figure.

7

Writing the Saints

What Hagiography is Not

Saints have a family of literature dedicated to them called hagiography, or 'writings about the holy'. The word is often used today to criticize biographers who lavish undue praise on their subjects, but this is a dilution of its original meaning. Hagiography straddles that familiar border between fiction and non-fiction. It has been the victim of Protestant confessional polemic and modern, scientific assumptions about what constitutes useful knowledge. Reform Protestants approach it with theological forbearance and find it full of superstition and dogma, a poor cousin of classical heroic mythology. Enlightened, secular sensibilities find sacred biography sterile and incredible, lacking in the celebration of individuality, moral ambiguity, and the psychological texture prized in modern biography.

We are bound to be disappointed if we read hagiography for empirical plausibility or historical accuracy. The purpose of hagiography was to find distinction not in the originality of a life but in its conformity to recognized types. The sixth-century Bishop Gregory of Tours entitled his collection of twenty holy biographies the *Life of the Fathers* to indicate that their 'merits and virtues', though distributed variously among them, shared a common origin in Christ. Writers and audiences of hagiography did not share the scientific convictions of moderns. They had not only expectations of the natural world but also an idea of how its envelopment in the supernatural had consequences for how humans should live.

Origins and Forms

Hagiography's roots were in classical forms of secular biography (panegyric, encomium, oration) and in the Gospels. It borrowed from the former all the persuasive techniques and forms used to describe the lives of extraordinary men and women, and from the latter it drew its central purpose and dramatic theme. The incarnation of Christ opened the way to God for Christians, and it was in imitation of Christ, interpreted and represented in multifarious ways by hagiography, that saints followed to salvation. The primary function of hagiography was to edify its audiences by exploring that living association between the particular and the eternal aspects of human experience. The narrative unit for this task was the life and memory of a saint. Hagiography identified in particular lives the signs of eternal holiness that would lift the souls and intellects of its readers and listeners heavenward. This is how the eleventh-century hagiographer, Goscelin of St Bertin put it in his proem to the miracles of St Aethelthryth of Ely:

> Let us strive to follow in the footsteps of saints in all
> things ... since they raise the minds of many who hear them
> from the depths to the heights, we ought most carefully to
> search out their miracles and outward signs ... and lest they
> slip from memory, to record them most wisely in books, and
> we ought also to place them in the closet of our heart by
> frequent reading, nor however, to contain them only within
> our walls, but also to proclaim them far and wide to the praise
> and glory of the Godhead, and for the edification of posterity.

Goscelin's manifesto followed the injunction of St Augustine
to keep little books of miracles (*libelli miraculorum*) at saints'
shrines for the benefit of posterity.

Hagiography is the greatest and most diverse literary legacy
of the medieval period. It was written in sacred languages,
Greek, Latin, Syriac, Coptic, Ge'ez, and in the vernacular. It
encompassed a range of sub-genres including saints' lives,
miracle collections, relic lists, deeds of the martyrs (*gesta
martyrum*), accounts of the miraculous discovery (*inventio*),
ritual translation (*translatio*), and elevation (*elevatio*) of saints'
relics, and martyrologies (in Orthodox and Eastern traditions,
the *menologion* or *synaxarion*).

Functions

Hagiography might be read alone, but it was more often
used in practical, communal situations. The liturgical sub-
genres served the cycle of divine worship in religious communities, so that excerpts from a saint's life might be read
out during divine office, the hours scheduled for daily prayer
in a monastery, on feast days, as lections or *legenda* (things

to be read), or, as prescribed in the Benedictine Rule, during mealtimes in the refectory. Hagiographers were skilled writers commissioned to preserve stories for edification and imitation. They helped in the promotion of posthumous cults by inventing and fixing institutional memories, often in competition with rival cult traditions. They supported cults liturgically and fostered wider devotional identities encompassing the custodians of relics and the lay clients of saintly patronage. Hagiography might serve other polemical or advocatory purposes, for example, in support of mission, to legitimize new hierarchies and claims to jurisdictional precedence or property rights. In short, hagiography linked the divine endorsement of the saints to all sorts of worldly causes.

Martyrologies

Martyrologies, or calendars, were records of saints arranged for liturgical purposes according to their official birthdays (*natales*), the dates of their birth as martyrs into everlasting heavenly glory. Medieval monastic communities would read out the names of the martyrs on their associated feast days. An early example of the genre was the *Hieronymian Martyrology* (named after its supposed author St Jerome) compiled in fifth-century Italy. Along with the name of the martyr it included the location of martyrdom. The eighth-century Northumbrian monk Bede introduced historical notes beside names in his martyrology, a development that caught on with subsequent compilers. Bede's martyrology served as the base for the landmark martyrology of Usuard, a late ninth-century monk of Saint-Germain-des-Prés. His work lay behind the universal *Roman Martyrology* of 1584. In the names they exclude and include, rather like modern lists of favourite English poems or pop songs, martyrologies, synaxeries, and menologia represent the living traditions of the Christian churches by subtly reflecting points of doctrinal and spiritual difference.

Gesta Martyrum

Martyrs were the earliest subjects of saintly biography. Commemoration of their lives in the *passio* (account of the suffering) or the *gesta martyrum* (deeds of the saints) conventionally included two dramatic set-piece scenes. First came the martyr's encounter with the authorities. The interrogation of the Christian by a Roman jurist enabled the narration of adversarial vignettes recalling Christ's cross-examination by Pontius Pilate in the Gospels. Hagiographers used the invented trial transcript to emphasize the integrity, heroism, and simplicity with which martyrs publicly bore witness to their faith. These qualities of steadfastness, composure, and simple abiding faith were consummated in the second climactic scene of narration, involving detailed description of the extreme violence the martyr suffered and serenely overcame at the point of death.

Saints' Lives

The most popular hagiographical sub-genre, the saint's life or *vita*, was traditionally commissioned as part of the preparation for episcopal translation, and later, papal canonization of a saint's relics, signalling their availability for public veneration. Most saints' lives were written after their death and not intended to flatter the subject. Sulpicius Severus wrote the *Life of St Martin* shortly before Martin's death, but it was not intended as a gift to its subject in anticipation of patronage. St Anselm discovered that his biographer, Eadmer, was keeping notes preparatory to the writing of his *vita*, and had him destroy them.

Saints' *vitae* have an episodic, static structure. There is little notion of character development, causation, or psychological motivation, or of chronological discontinuity; just a series of episodes upon which are piled moral and supernatural proofs of the saint's burgeoning holiness. Any number of the following scenes conventionally appear in a *vita*: the saint's birth is foretold in a vision or marked by some portent; the infant saint's precocious piety marks them out from their peer group; some event (the death of parents, the threat of arranged marriage, or a conversion experience) confirms the saint in their vocational path; their sanctity is demonstrated through vignettes illustrating the practical significance of their vocation as abbot, bishop, recluse, or virgin; their holiness is tested, progress is divinely rewarded and signalled by miracles (Latin *signa* or *miracula*) or abilities (prophecy, remote or heavenly visions, communication with wild animals, cursing and blessing); the saint predicts his or her own death; death is described intimately and at length; the saint's remains are ritually translated to a shrine, and posthumous miracles recorded. Accounts of the *translatio* or *miracula* became detached genres accompanying the *vita*.

A remarkable and relatively unknown branch of Christian hagiographical tradition is the two hundred or so *gädlat* (spiritual struggles of the saints literature) of the Ethiopian Täwahedo Church. The saints commemorated in this literary tradition, which spans from the fourteenth century to the nineteenth, tend to be monks, nuns, and evangelical priests. A rare translation into English of one of these texts is the *Gädla Walatta Petros*, perhaps the first biography of an African woman written by an African since the third-century *Passion of Perpetua and Felicity*. Written in the sacred script of Ethiopia, Ge'ez, the *gädl* genre features episodes familiar to readers of Greek and Latin hagiography but has its own conventions, for example, a scene called the *kidan*, in which the saint is depicted receiving a covenant from Christ, promising to answer the prayers of those who show devotion to the saint. A cherished musical form in Ethiopian Christian devotion is the *mälka*, or 'icon' poem, a rhythmic song praising in turn every minute part of a saint's body, from head to toes. The *Malka'a Maryam*, or image of the Virgin Mary, is sung in monasteries and households today in the Täwahedo Church.

Collections of Saints' Lives

There has been a perennial urge to collect the *Lives* of saints. The tenth-century Byzantine St Symeon Metaphrastes wrote a ten-volume collection of 150 saints' lives that brought older existing *legenda* together in a calendrical arrangement and in the latest prose style intended to ensure their preservation for the literary tastes of future audiences. Saints might be grouped in such collections according to type, or to represent the tastes of religious orders, or those of a particular geographical region, such as are reflected in the thirteenth-century 'South English Legendary'. Jacobus de Voragine's *Legenda Aurea* (The Golden Legend) is the most famous collection of saints' lives of any period. It survives in hundreds of manuscript copies, and in several vernacular editions, including Dutch, French, Old High German, Italian, Czech, and English.

Hagiographical Techniques

Hagiography developed through the creative elaboration of a narrow group of classical and late antique antecedents. We might see these interventions as pious invention in the service of devotional truth. The literary fabrication of hagiographical truth included the gradual exposition of a saintly ethos, the cultivation of a decorous style integral to the truth conveyed, the habitual referencing of canonical texts, and a robust sense of nature and its saturation in a supernatural reality discovered through the intellect. Its overall objective was to persuade by engaging the senses, the emotions, and the mind in a series of active responses, whether of contemplation or imitation, contrition or joy.

Intended to edify Christians and evangelize pagans, sacred biography was a serious undertaking for its practitioners. Authors employed a modesty *topos* (a commonplace or set-piece device) professing inadequacy to the task, and requesting the prayers of readers, their indulgence on matters of uncertainty, and assuring them that a pure motivation (not fame or financial compensation) appropriate to the subject treated lay behind their writing. The twelfth-century monk, Guibert of Nogent, associated sanctity with true writings (*scriptorium veracium*) that required not only reliable chains of eyewitness accounts but good style. Some biographers wrote 'worse than doggerel, unfit for the ears of swineherds', some in so 'ragged and pedestrian a style that by their awkwardness they defame the saints'.

The *Life of St Guthlac* (*Vita Sancti Guthlaci*) written by Felix, an eighth-century monk of Mercia, adapted elements from the *Lives* of Antony, Martin, and Cuthbert, and used biblical references, historical detail, and local stories from two named eyewitnesses, Abbot Wilfrid and Cissa, Guthlac's hermit successor. Its prologue includes a conventional apology from the author for his poor style: 'If...my faulty language shall here and there offend the ears of a learned reader...I ask his pardon...let him remember also...that the kingdom of God does not consist in the eloquence of our language but in the constancy of our faith.' Whatever it tells us about the author's self esteem, his humility prepared the reader to take responsibility for the content to follow by receiving it in a fitting manner.

Adomnán, the seventh-century abbot of Iona, used the same recursive technique in his preface to the *Life of St Columba*, drawing attention to his 'words, which I consider rough...' but recalling to his readers that 'the kingdom of God stands not on the flow of eloquence but in the flowering of faith'. Similar sentences appear in Sulpicius Severus's *Vita Martini*. Their common origin is 1 Corinthians 4.20.

We might suspect that *topoi* (commonplace stories) were sometimes used to fill the gaps in the author's knowledge of a saintly subject. Occasionally, authors admit to as much in comments to the effect that 'since such and such was this kind of saint, the fact that we have no record of him performing this miracle does not mean he did not perform it like this similar saintly precursor'. But through the use of *topoi*, regardless of their verifiability, the author also entrusted the reader with the devotional orientation of themselves towards the subject. What moderns might see as falsification was actually a literary bracketing device, a stimulus to the recalling of canonical models such as the *Lives* of St Antony, and St Martin, or the *Dialogues* of Gregory the Great. These *topoi* were creatively adapted to different historical circumstances. The adversarial role of Roman jurists in early martyr legends, for example, became that of demons in the *Life of St Antony*, and in the tenth-century poem, *Guthlac A*, that of besieging enemies and criminal outcasts.

Scholarly Criticism of Hagiography

Hagiography always had critics from within the tradition concerned with its proper practice. But doubts of its absolute worth set in during the late fifteenth century with its relative neglect by humanists more interested in classical literary forms, and in the following century, as one half of a divided Europe took leave of the cult of saints, and the practical and theological uses that hagiography supported. Reform Catholicism, in its new canonization procedures and emphasis on moral virtues and formal qualities of character over miracle-working and mystical virtuosity, also reined in the more fanciful content of medieval hagiography.

The serious scholarly return to hagiography began in the first half of the seventeenth century with the Bollandists, a Belgian school of Jesuits whose tradition was named after one of its founders, Jean Bolland (1596–1665). The early Bollandists pioneered critical editorial approaches to hagiography as part of a wider project of historical salvage that was characteristic of their age. They arranged medieval saints' lives into volumes organized comprehensively according to the calendar of saints' feast days. The project has continued (with one extended hiatus during the French revolutionary years) into the twenty-first century. Their scholarly techniques developed over this period, so that the combination of rational and apologetic aspects of editorial method changed.

English hagiology was less ambitious. Antiquarians and churchmen of the late seventeenth and early eighteenth centuries, 'men zealous for precedent and learned in its exposition', mined medieval manuscripts for answers to the constitutional problems of their day. Henry Wharton, a domestic chaplain in the household of Archbishop Sancroft, was one such man. Wharton's vision of an Anglican Church with apostolic authority represented by its bishops inspired him to collect the lives of saints associated with cathedral churches as part of his most famous work, the *Anglia Sacra*. His book brought to light the *Lives* of Wulfstan, Anselm, Gundulf of Rochester, Bregwine, and Oswald, though his confessional loyalties showed in his editorial excision of their miraculous content. But Wharton was unusual in his time for taking these sources seriously at all. Gilbert Burnet, bishop of Salisbury, was scornful:

> The barbarous Stile, the mixture of so much Fable, the great want of Judgement that runs through the writings of the Monks . . . If anyone that has more Patience than I can think it worth the while to search into that Rubbish, let him write volumes of *Anglia Sacra* and have the Glory of it for his Pains.

Wharton's work in reviving memories of the saints in England was taken up by Cardinal Newman as part of that mission of the nineteenth-century Oxford Movement to restore some wonder and mysticism to the Anglican Church. Ironically, scholarship in the Roman Catholic Church was at this time engaged in just the opposite undertaking.

Hippolyte Delehaye

The Bollandist Hippolyte Delehaye published his state of the art method on hagiological criticism, *Les Légendes Hagiographiques*, in 1905. As well as an important introductory textbook, it put the study of hagiography, and with it the veneration of saints, on scientific grounds. Delehaye stripped legend from sacred biography like barnacles from the hull of a boat. His method eschewed local cult traditions and insisted on the interrogation of hagiography for evidence of myth-making, legend, fable, and tale. He found errors in transcription and translation, and the linguistic puns hagiographers made (St Clare improves your eyesight!) that resulted in the fabrication of fictional saints or the attachment of legend to old ones.

Delehaye attributed the largest number of legendary accretions not to well-intentioned or incompetent hagiographers but to the collective authorization of the faithful masses. The 'unsophisticated mind of the people' is a frequent patsy in Delehaye's exposition of erroneous hagiographical tradition. It is intellectually infantile, easily distracted by objects, credulous, especially when flattered, disproportionately emotional, given to fantasy and wonder, but languishing under the poverty of invention. Delehaye's removal of all the populist plaque from the genre leaves one wondering what value remains in the historical fact uncovered. It certainly spared the blushes of those young seminarians embarrassed by the clash of modern science with their liturgical observance of the saints. We can guess his disciplined apology for the cult of saints made satisfying reading for the tidier-minded, but was perhaps rather too high and dry for the more spirited and romantic of the Catholic laity. In any case, the legends lived on and even Delehaye conceded that some of them did so justifiably given their poetic beauty.

Aside from its invaluable testimony to religious practice, ecclesiastical, political, and social history, hagiography's longevity and variety has made it a vast storehouse of human understandings and expressions of spirituality, and of the relationship between God, the saints, and humanity. Hagiography's enduring presence in between the spirituality and self-help sections of bookshops is proof that the ancient provenance of its forms and conventions continues to inspire new readers.

8

Globalizing Sanctity

The cult of saints crossed global horizons as part of the spread of Roman Catholicism that accompanied what world historians call the occidental breakout. The breakout began in the late fifteenth century with the maritime expeditions of Catholic Portugal and Spain. The Portuguese opened up routes, via Africa, to Brazil and Goa and Calicut on the west coast of India, and beyond to Indonesia, the Spice Islands, China, and Japan. The Spanish colonized South America, parts of southern North America, the Caribbean, and coastal islands off Africa, and the Philippines.

Mission and Sainthood

In all these places the cult of saints gained a foothold as part of the religious mission of the Europeans. The Church was relatively muted on the conduct of world mission. Previous popes had tied its hands by granting the imperial rulers of the Iberian Peninsula full jurisdiction, the *patronata* (*patroado* in Portuguese), over ecclesiastical organization abroad.

The mendicant orders were often the earliest to minister to the native populations, but the Society of Jesus (the

Jesuits) was the nearest the Church came to centrally orchestrated global mission. St Francis Xavier, a founding member of the Jesuits, arrived in Japan in 1549 in the early days of what proved to be an unsuccessful Christian mission there. The civil war in Japan of the second half of the sixteenth century was won by the Tokugawa dynasty. The new regime embraced a Buddhist political culture, persecuted Jesuits and mendicants at court, and among their local Christian congregations, eradicating the priesthood and driving Christian communities underground.

Jesuit martyrdoms in Japan, the Philippines, and Canada became a powerful recruitment tool for pious young men in Europe. Wall paintings of the martyrs brought inspirational stories of mission into the living space of the Sant' Andrea al Quirinale noviciate in Rome, whilst the ambulatory frescoes of Rome's San Stefano Rotondo depicting early church martyrs, and a book containing engraved reproductions of them, through their evocation of the Catholic Church triumphant, fed the spiritual imaginations of young Jesuit missionaries to Germany and beyond. Similar engravings were distributed, according to an annal from the English Jesuit College in Rome '...even to the Indies, that the infamy of this most disastrous persecution, the frenzied rage of the heretics, the unconquerable firmness of the Catholics, may be known everywhere'.

The Americas

At the far western extreme of the European breakout, the most successful seedbed of sainthood was the Americas.

There, the Church received most patronage when it operated as an ideological arm of colonial government, working to pacify and economically exploit the Amerindian natives. By 1620, there were thirty-six bishoprics, two universities, and four hundred priories in New Spain. Positions in the church were drawn from the creoles (American-born Iberians) and the *peninsulares* (new Iberian arrivals). The Amerindians were excluded from ordained positions in the church, though they could serve in the liturgy and in tertiary religious institutions.

Colonial Sainthood

The European habit of labelling as 'New' that part of the world it encountered after Columbus's famous crossing of the Atlantic in 1492 has privileged colonial perspectives of that historical encounter ever since. It reinforced territorial claims, gave the impression that these worlds were 'box fresh', waiting to be possessed, and ignored all that historically preceded the advent of Europeans in the land. The *conquistadores* treated the Indios harshly. The *encomienda* system legally enforced a kind of medieval serfdom in which communities were tied to land as units of labour 'entrusted' to Spanish soldiers, administrators, and churchmen. Forced labour in the silver mines of Potosí (modern Bolivia) was even worse. Smallpox reduced the immunologically vulnerable population to almost ten per cent of its original level by 1650. The consolidation of plantation economies fed by slaves abducted from Africa brings more texture to our understanding of the word 'New' in this colonial setting.

In these miserable conditions, we might ask why the indigenous people adopted the religion of their Christian oppressors and what part saints played in that process? The brief answers are because there was little else they could do, and that saints were an important channel of communication and authority for natives otherwise excluded from ordination and office. A brief survey of the saints who emerged from these protracted encounters suggests a dynamic situation on the ground in which colonial sainthood took the metropolitan Catholicism of the Tridentine Church and transformed it to suit local conditions. The Americas were inhabited by old civilizations (the Incas and Aztecs), hunter-gatherers, and nomadic warriors, all with their own religious specialists, cultures, and rituals, and, joined by the religions of Africa, they brought their own novelty to an Old World phenomenon.

For over a century Potosí was the engine of a new world economy, its chief raw material driving an accelerating carousel of commodities between Europe and silver-hungry China in the Far East. It is perhaps no surprise to note that in such circumstances arose a devotional fondness for the Virgin Mary. A sumptuous eighteenth-century painting, *La Virgen del Cerro Rico* (see Figure 10), depicts the Virgin in a dress that is also Cerro Rico, the silver mountain of Potosí. Embroidered on its foothills and ascents are native mineworkers supervised by an Inca ruler. In the foreground of the image are its European patrons, among them Pope Paul II and Emperor Charles V. In this painting the Virgin is a model of syncretic sanctity, replacing Pachamama, the Andean goddess traditionally associated with Mother Nature, as protector and creator of bounty.

Figure 10 *La Virgen del Cerro Rico*, oil on canvas, eighteenth century, anonymous. *Casa Nacional de Moneda, Potosí, Bolivia.*

Syncretic Sanctity

A fundamental feature of Catholic world mission was syncretism, the mixing of elements of two sets of religious belief and meaning through the adaptation of symbols and practices culturally accommodating to both. In these syncretic conditions, dogma alternated with improvisation, and the simple desire for human association and understanding occasionally registered a foothold on a mental landscape of racial prejudice, and fear borne out of exploitation.

The chief agents and agencies of syncretism on the one hand were those of the mendicant religious orders and the Jesuits, some the product of settler marriages with native families. A remarkable example was the Dominican and early colonial bishop, Bartolomé de Las Casas, whose several writings revealed the degree and character of destruction wrought on indigenous peoples, and who began to articulate a theory of racial equality and native rights in response to it. On the other hand were indigenous converts seeking protection, status, and a voice in the new colonial environment. The aspects of Christian practice that were more accessible and familiar to such groups, especially when they were barred from ordination, were the charismatic leadership of religious men and women, and saintly patronage.

New Spain

In New Spain, the Jesuits and Dominicans learned native languages to aid catechism and confession, and adopted Nahuatl, a *lingua franca*, to convey doctrine in writing. The indigenous faithful gradually learned Christian doctrine and practice, and were given public roles in ceremonies and festivals that echoed pre-existing traditions of religious observance. When the beatification of Ignatius Loyola was celebrated at the Jesuit headquarters in Cuzco, Peru, in 1610, the figures of eleven Inca monarchs were paraded and their portraits subsequently displayed on the walls of the college.

The seventeenth-century creole Jesuit Antonio Ruiz de Montoya (d.1652) worked among the Guaraní people of Paraguay. His book, *La Conquista Espiritual del Paraguay*, gives an account of Jesuit mission to, and settlement of, the native Guaraní people in *reducciones*, the new settlements in cleared areas of forest. One historian has noted how the Jesuits competed with the local forest shamans for the devotional attentions of the Guaraní. They blessed statues the Guaraní brought them in which were hidden amulets dedicated to San La Muerte, a death figure of local folk religion. But they also tracked down the shrines of forest shamans and had them destroyed. In 1628, Roque González de Santa Cruz, a Jesuit missionary of Spanish noble descent, was killed by a local shaman, Nehcu. He was beatified in 1634 and canonized in Asunción, Paraguay, by Pope John Paul II in 1988.

The most famous example of syncretism in New Spain is the cult of Our Lady of Guadalupe in Tepeyac, Mexico City. Its origins in the first two or three decades of Spanish settlement are obscure, but clearly rose out of an indigenous religious enthusiasm lately acknowledged by the Church. The story surfaces in the mid-seventeenth-century account by a creole priest, Miguel Sánchez, of Juan Diego, a poor

Amerindian instructed in 1531 by the Virgin in a vision to build a chapel in her honour in Tepeyac (the cult site of Tonantzin, an Aztec mother god). It took a series of further visions, in one of which his cape became imprinted with the image of the Virgin left by mountain flowers, and a miracle, before Juan Diego could convince his bishop to build a chapel. Women were often conduits and interpreters of native culture in association with male religious authorities. The Americas' first canonized saint (in 1671) was St Rosa of Lima (d.1617), daughter of a Spanish military family, who died aged thirty-one after a life of asceticism, penance, and local charity in emulation of the medieval Dominican tertiary, St Catherine of Siena.

New England

North America was colonized by Protestant Europe in the seventeenth century, in three areas: Chesapeake Bay, in what became Maryland and Virginia; New Amsterdam, later New York; and the Massachusetts Bay Colony of Boston and New England. Those who arrived in New England were Puritans breaking away from the intolerable compromises they associated with Anglicanism. They sought to institute in New England a Church of the godly elect, a community of saints like that of the primitive Pauline church. In the absence of immediate monarchical or ecclesiastical authority, the congregation of saints forged itself from a combination of civic authority and mutual, communal moral scrutiny. The early churches of New England were sectarian; they defined themselves against inferior Christians of universal churches, and, in their efforts to resemble that heavenly community of the righteous predestined, they excluded those whose moral behaviour fell short of what they considered visible sanctity. The temptation of persecution's former victims to persecute got the better of the Massachusetts Bay Colony. Between 1659 and 1661 they executed four Quakers for heresy and witchcraft in a rare sequence of martyrdoms at the hands of saints. Among them was Mary Dyer, executed on Boston Common in June 1660. Her relative anonymity today reflects a Quaker reluctance to celebrate martyrdom, certainly at least in anything other than its broadest spiritual terms as a kind of pain that any of the faithful might endure graciously and without fuss.

New France

The St Lawrence River links the Great Lakes of the American Midwest with the Atlantic Ocean and now defines the border between USA and Canada. It was named by the sixteenth-century French explorer Jacques Cartier. The regions it opened up to European colonization (upstate New York, the St Lawrence Valley, and the Finger Lakes) were claimed as New France in the seventeenth century. The Jesuits undertook missionary work there from 1615 among the peoples of the Iroquois Nation and other Amerindians. The Huron–Iroquois Wars of 1642–9 resulted in the terrible martyrdom of eight Jesuits, captured and tortured to death by native Americans. Isaac Jogues was slain by Mohawks in the mission settlement of Auriesville in 1646. Also among them was St Jean de Brébeuf, responsible for modern Canada's beloved 'Huron Carol', which he wrote in the native writing system he helped to devise. Jean de Brébeuf contributed material to *Jesuit Relations,* a sequence of multiple-authored ethnographical reports collected over forty years, of Jesuit encounters with native communities. The work contains purported eyewitness accounts of his torture and execution. All eight Jesuits were canonized in 1930.

The story of Jean de Brébeuf and his saintly companions inspired the Frenchman Claude Chauchetière to become a Jesuit in Canada, where, in 1677, he arrived at a mission station called Kahnawake. The same year, Catherine Tekakwitha, a young Mohawk convert to Christianity, and born in the village where Isaac Jogues had been martyred ten years before, arrived at Kahnawake. Her life and death at the mission station two years later inspired miracles, a shrine, and early public veneration only recently acknowledged by Rome, where she was canonized in October 2012. Chauchetière was the chief early advocate of this 'savage saint', writing her biography by *c.*1690. Her asceticism, heroic virginity, and mystical powers, as retold by her Jesuit confessors, made her a fitting successor to her medieval Sienese namesake. But enough contradiction and 'spin' emerges from the historical record to suspect that Catherine, and the native female companions with whom she shared the religious life, were not passive imitators of medieval models of sanctity nor easy for the Jesuits to handle, but imaginative spiritual bricoleurs. Their desire to become a religious order led them beyond Jesuit prescription and expectation, and their willingness to repurpose native culture, for example in undergoing extreme suffering as part of their ascetic discipline, startled their Jesuit confessors.

It was customary of Iroquois peoples, by torturing their captives, to offer them a chance through a final show of bravery to nullify the shame of captivity. Self-torture was a practical way of preparing for the possibility of capture, but such violence also had a sacred dimension to it compatible with Catholic ascetic practice. Accounts of Iroquois warriors eating Jesuit hearts imply they shared a degree of admiration for the stoical suffering of their Christian captives. Physical suffering was a meaningful way for Catherine to test her own progress in the faith, by imitating the flagellation, fasting, and sleep deprivation practised by the Ursuline hospital nuns, and improvising native variations on them. Catherine punctured her whole body by rolling around in thorn bushes, exposed herself to extremes of temperature, walking barefoot on the ice, and applying firebrands to the skin between her toes whilst saying the *Ave Maria*; she dislocated her shoulders and, when not fasting, mixed ash into her food. It all won her the baffled awe of her Jesuit confessors, schooled in a European assumption of the savage woman as a dumb slave to sexual compulsions.

Africa

The kingdom of Kongo was converted under Portuguese missionary influence by King Afonso I (1509–43). Afonso had defeated his brother after invoking St James 'Matamoros' on the battlefield. Kongolese Catholicism endured into the eighteenth century as a mix of Catholicism and the native folk ritual of *kindoki*. Because the Kongolese ruling elite impeded European control of its ecclesiastical structures, and Portuguese involvement in the slave trade undermined the moral status of its clergy, the established Kongolese Catholicism was highly Africanized. When the state lapsed into protracted civil war after the 1660s, a peculiarly African form of charismatic Christian leadership provided a focus for peace and unity around the cult of a young Kongolese woman, Dona Beatriz Kimpa Vita. Beatriz Kimpa Vita was an *nganga*, a spirit medium in the *kindoki* tradition, until 1704, when, inspired by Capuchin missionaries, she announced herself to have died, been resurrected, and possessed by St Anthony of Padua. Beatriz went on to mobilize a popular religious movement, the Antonians, on the strength of a revelation entrusted to her that Jesus, Mary, and St Francis had all been Kongolese.

The Antonians occupied the war-torn capital of São Salvador, before one of the disputing kings in the civil war captured and burned their 'living dead' leader for heresy and witchcraft in 1706. Beatriz's cult has been interpreted by turns as a peace movement, an anti-slavery movement, and an anti-colonial religious movement. It certainly represents another example of Africa's great religious creativity. Antonianism resurfaced in the North American colonies when, in 1739, Catholic Kongolese slaves broke their chains at Stono Bridge in South Carolina in a bid for liberty in Spanish Florida. Ironically, in Brazil, St Anthony of Padua had already acquired quite a different reputation. He was the recoverer of lost objects, and specifically for *mamelucos*, or slave-hunters, of runaway slaves. Portuguese colonials also called upon him as a military saint in the blessing of fortresses.

The African noblewoman Walatta Petros (d.1642) is the most historically prominent among a number of Habasa noblewomen of the Täwahedo Christian Church of highland Ethiopia. The depiction of these women in Western accounts, and in Walatta Petros's case in her own biography written within thirty years of her death, clearly indicates their dogged leadership of native Christian resistance to the proto-colonial mission of Portuguese-backed Jesuits. The centralizing and hierarchical refinements that Roman Catholicism brought to political authority in the region help to explain the protection and endowment it received from early seventeenth-century Habasa kings. To frustrate this emerging alliance, however, several high-status noblewomen gained a reputation in Portuguese accounts as highly literate, obstinate heretics, annoyingly skilled at public disputation, and at cursing. The *Gädla Walatta Petros*, or 'life-struggles of the spiritual daughter of Peter', preserves an image of its heroine as a model of asceticism, a founder of monasteries, and reformer of religious life, and as a mother figure and intercessor for the native Christian faithful. On one occasion in her biography Walatta Petros is summoned to court to dispute with 'three renowned European false teachers ... about their filthy faith'. Her response is succinctly recorded: 'she argued with them, defeated them ... laughed and made fun of them'.

Modern Syncretic Sanctity

Other examples of Christian syncretism, among them *Candomblé* in Brazil, and *Santería* in the Caribbean, operate beyond official approval and submerge African cosmologies in outwardly Catholic rituals; the identities of the *orishas*, or deities, of the Yoruba tradition, for example, are blurred into those of familiar Catholic saints. The cult of Santa Muerte, or St Death, has flourished over the last two decades among Mexicans in Central and North America. Devotion to the 'Bony Lady' has obscure roots in the colonial period, but the scale of its current resurgence is unprecedented. In association with the Mexican government the Catholic Church has raised concern for the cult's demonic aspects and stressed its associations with narcotics trafficking and gang culture. Wayside shrines have been bulldozed, and attempts to secure its official recognition by the Church spurned. Still, it exists in a variety of benign everyday settings for its devotees, who light differently coloured candles to secure one form of assistance or another from the saint.

9

Saints in the Modern World

The late seventeenth century through to the eighteenth is traditionally seen as the moment of intellectual foment that led Europe into the modern, secular world. There is good reason to adopt this view. This was an age of intellectual experimentation and enquiry inspired by new kinds of association (professional bodies, royal academies, business associations, and freemasonry) operating beyond church and state. Europe had learned from its religious and civil wars and was becoming an optimistic society buoyed by its trading connections with the world. Protestant England and the Netherlands led the way as states tolerant of free thought and conscience. It is tempting to think of these developments as a victory for science and reason over religion and revelation, as a radical shift from enchantment to objectivity, from providence to progress, and a liberation from the hierarchical *ancien régime* of Church, absolutist monarchy, and unwarranted deference to old dogma; in short, as heralding a world of equality between men (not yet women) where the rational individual supplanted the saint as a model of human accomplishment.

But this picture is only partially true. First, it privileges the perspectives of a literate few in an emergent, urban bourgeois. Second, the period was one of not only enlightenments but also entanglements between intellectual advocates across the notional divide of faith and reason, religious custom, and scientific progress. The natural philosophers and freethinkers, such as John Toland (d.1722) and Pierre Bayle (d.1706), were often not atheists but deists, who arrived at the existence of God by ways that left little space for sacred scripture, god-men, or virgin births, still less for saints. They wrestled, nevertheless, with enduring theological debates about man in relation to God and Nature, original sin, freewill and salvation, about human consciousness and epistemology (the study of what can be known and how it can be known), and whether understanding comes from reason or emotion. For example, John Locke privileged sense perceptions, or the empirical method, over those truths revealed through priestly ritual and the calendar customs provided by saints' feast days. The saints in David Hume's *Natural History of Religion*—an innovative explanation of religion, written without reference to Christianity's self-validating biblical or doctrinal claims—were godlings, degrading objects of polytheist superstition, their miracles no proof of divine intervention. Men like Newton took a more moderate position, confidently exploring the world afresh with a presumption that their experimentation revealed natural laws enacted by the Creator of an ordered universe.

The familiar textbook stories of endemic nepotism, greed, ignorance, and moral scandal in the eighteenth-century Roman Catholic Church, of atheist bishops and licentious aristocrat monks and priests, are testimony in part to the rhetorical virtuosity of the French *philosophes*, men like Diderot, Voltaire, and Montesquieu. Their anticlerical intellectualism, however, needs to be weighed against a progressive tendency among intellectuals within the Church inspired by reason and moral ambition to reform ecclesiastical institutions, to educate the priesthood, and minister to the faithful.

Canonizations continued throughout the Enlightenment period, though not in great numbers. Twenty-four were canonized in the seventeenth century and twenty-nine in the eighteenth. These new saints tended to cut fairly conventional figures, reflecting an ecclesiastical approach tempered by moderation and reason. They were predominantly male, secular clergy or avowed religious, and often founders of monastic orders. Among the latter, for example, were Teresa of Ávila, Filippo Neri, and Ignatius Loyola (all canonized in 1622), and Vincent de Paul (canonized in 1737). They were largely Italian, Spanish, or French, of noble and middling status, and engaged in mission or charitable work among the poor. They tended to be canonized a century or more after their lifetimes, their reputation for sanctity long established or else too remote to be contested. They were candidates whose sanctity sat well with moderate Enlightenment values; there were few martyrs, great theologians, or mystics among them.

Some enlightened reforms were popular, but others reflected a heightened distaste for folk religion. Pope Pius

VI (d.1799) founded the Vatican Museum as an important destination in a new kind of pilgrimage—tourism. The Holy Roman Emperor Joseph II of Austria (d.1790) introduced new standards of pastoral care, training for the priesthood, and oversight of monastic discipline, dissolving some monasteries and establishing new seminaries. Grand Duke Leopold of Tuscany (d.1792) sponsored Scipio de Ricci, bishop of Pistoia and Prato, in banning the cult of the Sacred Heart, devotional stations, processions, and indulgences. Statues were removed from churches, and the breviary pruned of extraneous legends. When in May 1787 the people of Prato rioted at rumours that the Girdle of the Blessed Virgin was earmarked for destruction, the reforms soon gave way to brutal oppression before then petering out.

The rationalization of religion was driven to its logical conclusion by the French Revolution's attempt in the 1790s to de-Christianize the Republic and replace Catholicism with the Cult of Reason, a civic religion celebrating French Enlightenment values. On 3 December 1793, civic officials burned the relics of St Genevieve, patron saint of Paris, melted down her reliquary, and threw her ashes in the Seine. The newly built church, once awaiting its dedication to her, had already been re-conceived as the Panthéon, and housed the remains of Voltaire. The trouble was, earlier in the Revolution the common Parisian folk had enlisted St Genevieve to the revolutionary cause. Garlands had been laid at her shrine, *ex-votos* offered, and popular liturgical innovations introduced. As a result the cult outlived the Revolution thanks to the resilience of this local, lived religion. New relics were discovered in the church of St-Étienne-du-Mont, and public veneration resumed with *ex-votos* being placed by her tomb.

Where Enlightenment abstraction, whether serving or in lieu of the Church, failed to beguile the people, nineteenth-century industrialization wrought new disruptions upon traditional society. A mass migration of the people into urban wage-labour and the subjection of the rural population to new work disciplines and relative impoverishment allowed the papacy to settle down into a populist authoritarian berth, as the consoler of the people and protector of venerable religious customs. Landmark papal rulings of the age included official acknowledgement of the Immaculate Conception in 1854, the publication of the 'Syllabus of Errors' in 1864, Pope Pius IX's statement of profound intransigence towards modernizing forces in the world, and the declaration of Papal Infallibility of 1870.

We have already seen evidence of populism in the Church's positive response to Marian visions reported by rural peasant communities. In Italy and England, the cult of Aloysius Gonzaga served similar spiritual inclinations. Aloysius Gonzaga, a Jesuit recruit of the highest breeding, died in 1591 aged twenty-four, tending to the poor victims of a plague in Rome. He was canonized in 1726. Initially a model of chaste adolescence, Gonzaga's memory became hitched in the 1860s to 'Catholic Action', a conservative Italian youth movement that made of the aristocratic Jesuit an emblem of religious patriotism. His irresistibly romantic story also won for Aloysius the devotion of sensitive-minded adolescent congregants at the eponymously dedicated Jesuit parish church of Oxford, founded in 1875 (and now known as the Oxford Oratory).

England

Anglicanism has retained a habit of devotion to saints in its annual calendar of holy days. The 'holy days of Anglican saints and heroes' listed in the *Calendar of Common Worship* overlap with some found in Roman Catholicism but others recognize saints venerated in the various provinces particular to the Anglican Communion. Alongside St Antony of Egypt, the venerable Bede, St Dunstan, and St Augustine sit the Reformation martyrs, King Charles I, the social reformer Josephine Butler, and the romantic poet, Christina Rossetti (author of the popular Christmas carol, *In the Bleak Midwinter*). The martyrs' memorial above the great door of Westminster Abbey commemorates ten martyrs of the twentieth century, including Maximilian Kolbe, Dietrich Bonhoeffer, Martin Luther King Jr, Óscar Romero, and Manche Masemola, the South African girl murdered by her parents in 1928 for seeking baptism at her local Christian mission run by the Anglican Community of the Resurrection. Though the Church of England formally rejects the notion, the more Catholic among its worshipers do prayerfully petition saints in the hope of intercession.

Russia

At the eastern edges of Enlightenment Europe, the Russian despots, Peter the Great (d.1725) and Catherine the Great (d.1796), introduced Western reforms to the Russian Orthodox Church, including in 1725 the replacement of the

Patriarchate at its apex with a Holy Synod, effectively making the Orthodox Church an arm of imperial authority. Also out of these reforms developed an educated metropolitan and episcopal elite made up of monks often operating across huge diocesan territories, and—remote from ecclesiastical supervision—an uneducated local priesthood that customarily married and passed parish livings down through their families. A different type of sainthood to that of Western Europe emerged out of these circumstances, one fostered in provincial monasteries where feats of asceticism and eremitical observance, in the absence of a motivated local priesthood, directly inspired and protected the faithful. St Tikhon of Zadonsk (d.1783) was a monk of peasant stock from Novgorod, who rose to become bishop of Voronezh. His early retirement from the bishopric in all likelihood resulted from a tireless commitment to his pastoral duties. He was a particularly gifted popular religious educator, preacher, and advocate of the discipline of profound spiritual self-examination. One of his popular pamphlets of spiritual instruction, *Attend to Oneself*, launches a relentless battery of moral impugnments at the Christian reader, each punctuated by the intimidating refrain 'Attend to yourself' (see Figure 11). The *starets* was an elder figure within monastic culture, a charismatic virtuoso in hesychastic techniques of prayer rooted in medieval Greek orthodoxy, and revived in eighteenth-century Russia. St Seraphim of Sarov (d.1833) was the most famous Russian *starets* of the period. A hermit, a healer, and a prophet, he was glorified in the Orthodox Church in 1903.

Figure 11 St Tikhon of Zadonsk icon, eighteenth-century Russian Orthodox.

North America

A peculiar combination of esoteric and primitive Pauline ideals of sainthood gained revelatory momentum in the second half of the nineteenth century to those who followed Joseph Smith and then Brigham Young west from New England and Ohio ultimately to settle on a section of the Rocky Mountains. The Church of Jesus Christ of Latter-day Saints received their revelation from the Book of Mormon, discovered written on golden tablets by the movement's Moses figure, Joseph Smith, after a tip-off from an angel called Moroni. The great book restored knowledge of a lost tribe of Christ's American followers, and foretold their revival in a mass religious movement of latter-day saints. An inspired variety of the kind of spiritual entrepreneurship that helped build the nation, Smith's Mormonism barrelled and barnstormed its way across America before making its present home in Salt Lake City, Utah.

The Twentieth Century: No More Heroes?

For most of the twentieth century the Roman Catholic Church canonized relatively few saints, perhaps understandably given the demoralizing circumstances. Intellectually, Darwinism had replaced the story of sanctification through ascent to the divine with one of man's descent from monkeys. In fashioning its own myths, Freudian psychology had drawn upon Greek rather than Christian human drama. Nietzsche's *Genealogy of Morals* had depicted the saint not as a model for imitation but as the emblem

145

of a 'slave morality'. When his antihero Zarathustra was asked for an offering from a hermit-saint he encountered in the forest he responded: 'What could I have to give you? But let me go quickly lest I take something from you.'

In public life, science and liberal constitutionalism prized principles of equal access to knowledge, public utility, and individualism over a hierarchy of humanity calibrated by moral and spiritual proximity to God. With catastrophic results, Communism and National Socialism put the cult of personality to the service of unspeakably evil political ideologies. The two World Wars brought unprecedented pessimism to the question of humanity's potential for good, and left some Christian apologists pondering where was God. Today, the cult of celebrity repackages charisma as a form of commoditized *schadenfreude*, hoisting pop stars, sportsmen and -women, and movie idols up on pedestals only to bring them crashing down as the often tragic consequences of their lives of excess and transgression play out. A curious parallel exists between the frequent death of young saints at the age of twenty-four, and the likes of Janis Joplin, Jimi Hendrix, Jim Morrison, Kurt Cobain, and Amy Winehouse, all known for their tragic early deaths as members of the '27 Club'.

After Sainthood

Between the 1940s and the late 1980s, Catholic writing about saints took an elegiac tone in a world seemingly 'after sainthood'. The sociologist of religion, John A. Coleman mourned a 'cultural numbness' and 'disarray' in the absence of modern hagiography and theological interest in saints, in the lack of a living conversation about them, and a loss of appropriate language to fire that conversation. His defence of sainthood was also an indictment of secular modernity with its 'utilitarianism and expressive individualism', rejection of moral hierarchy, and assault on tradition. Participation in 'communities of memory', a sense of 'God's concrete providence', and a 'resource of altruistic behaviour' were what stood to be gained from a renewed enthusiasm for the saints. Coleman reminded his readers of the Thomist distinction between Aristotelian virtues acquired by mastery, and the heroic Christian virtues of Faith, Hope, and Charity, bestowed upon the saints by God. Finally, he recommended that 'We must elevate talk about saints to the status of "serious discourse".'

Lived Religion

There is undoubtedly something valid in Coleman's observations. They were borne out by the experience of William A. Christian when in 1988 he returned to the Spanish valley in which he had conducted fieldwork in 1968–9 to find changes in the devotional landscape. On his first visit there had been a busy network of chapels and shrines containing images and relics that had activated memories, affirmed identities, and maintained a thousand different intimate associations between families, neighbours, individuals, and the saints after whom they were named. Peasant women called names like Carmen, Assumpta, Concepción, and Pilar were the nervous system of such crucial forms of local association between heaven and earth. But by 1988, the number of priests had declined from seven to two, and commemoration of the dead, and the naming of women by Marian aliases, along with church attendance, had all declined.

On the other hand, it might be suggested that Coleman's views share the cerebral predispositions of secular writers, both being part of that entanglement of Enlightenment with theological reasoning. Whilst secularists wait forlornly for the terminal eclipse of religious superstition, the danger is that religious apologists look for a definitional neatness to the cult of saints the absence of which in lived religion they mistake for decline rather than creative difference. In fact, secularization eroded some forms of popular devotion to the saints, but the need for saints has never left local Catholic communities, and has endured, adapted, and remained buoyant in constantly changing cultural, social, and geographical surroundings. Among generations of European Catholics moving to the USA after the First World War, for example, or following the arrival of Latino and Hispanic Catholics there from South America, devotion to saints has remained in rude health. Saints relocate with their migrant clients, new saints like Santa Muerte in Mexico and North America rise in popularity, and very old saints are rescued from historical obscurity as communities rediscover their pasts in an emerging post-secular world.

The modern Catholic Church hesitantly swung between its liberal modernizers and populist conservative wings during these decades, until one towering figure saw the cult of saints as a chance to revive ecclesiastical confidence in God's presence through the lives of saints.

The Return of the Saint: Pope John Paul II (1978–2005)

One hundred and fifty-eight saints were made between 1846 and 1978. Since then more than a thousand saints have been canonized and a small army of the beatified await promotion to full cult status upon their completion of a second miracle. One of them, Edith Stein, was a feminist philosopher and convert from Judaism to the religious habit of a Discalced Carmelite. The Nazis murdered her at Auschwitz in 1942. Her beatification as a martyr in 1987, and canonization in 1998 following her performance of a miracle, was seen as hasty given the technicalities of the case. Some considered it unclear, unlikely even, that the Nazis murdered her for her Christian faith rather than for her Jewish descent. The fact of her conversion moreover made her stated death 'for all Jews' an unwelcome opening for Christian proselytizing to them. The immensely popular Padre Pio (d.1968), Capuchin priest of Apulia, who exhibited the stigmata, could read hearts in the confessional, perform miracle cures, prophesy, and even bilocate, was for some time too embarrassingly 'medieval' a saint for the modern Church. Nevertheless, he was canonized in 2002. Both were remarkable characters, their common destiny sealed by their link to Bishop Karol Wojtyla of Kraków, in whose diocese Stein was murdered, and whose rise to the pontificate Padre Pio is attributed with having predicted when the holy mystic met with the Polish priest-pilgrim in 1947.

John Paul II was the first great canonizing pope of the modern age. He canonized 483 saints during his pontificate, more than all his predecessors combined. The first non-Italian Pope for centuries, he became the most-travelled Pope ever. He lived through Nazi and Communist regimes, and was committed to spreading a worldwide message of Christian hope and love. John Paul II's beatification of 1,341 holy men and women bears out the comment attributed by Kenneth Woodward, an expert on modern saint-making, to Archbishop Crisan, secretary of the Congregation for the Causes of Saints that 'When he travels, the Pope likes to bring a blessed in his pocket.'

In 1983, John Paul II devolved to his bishops the initiative for the framing of deserving causes in a collection of reforms that accelerated canonization procedures. Under those reforms the Sacred Congregation for the Causes of Saints in the Vatican, guided by a team of relators, now produces a *positio* (a dossier including a biography and evidence of heroic virtue and miracles) out of materials supplied by local bishops, for consideration by the Pope. There is no 'devil's advocate' or adversarial function in this legal process any-more, and only one miracle need qualify a candidate for beatification, a further one for canonization. Those of Pope John Paul II's canonized saints who are not martyrs tend to be male (and if female then nuns), ordained, and founders of religious orders, missionaries, or teachers. French, Spanish, and Italian saints still dominate the list.

Frustrations exist at the way the system exhibits self-selection bias, that is, a willingness of its functionaries to identify saints from among their own clerical and spiritual worldview. A good example of this is Josemaría Escrivá de Balaguer, founder of Opus Dei, who died in 1975 and was canonized in 2002. Opus Dei is an organization dedicated to the idea that holiness can be found in the lives of the most ordinary of the laity. It operates, however, outside the episcopal administration as a rather secretive international society, some say sect, grounded in populist conservative Catholicism, with little check on its activities. The proportion of those hundreds of cardinals, archbishops, bishops, and clergy who showed a special interest by petitioning with letters for their causes and who were also members of Opus Dei is not known.

Conversely, John Paul's antipathy towards liberation theology left Óscar Romero out of the reckoning for years, after he was assassinated at his altar in 1980 for denouncing the regime in El Salvador. The local postulator began collecting evidence in 1990, but the case was effectively suspended indefinitely until 2012. He was only beatified in May 2015, a year after the canonization of Pope John Paul II himself.

Canonization has proven an immensely useful instrument of papal policy, providing a rationale for evangelizing, a chance to publicize local devotions, and to communicate the relevance of sanctity in the world today. But the use of canonization by John Paul II has produced a predictable (if occasionally eccentric) cohort of new saints. There are misgivings about the unevenness of modern canonization procedures, for example, the success rate of religious institutions which have the most resources to throw at the process and the most to gain from canonization of their founders, or the fact that popes can exercise considerable discretion

Figure 12 A modern bahitawi 'hermit monk', Ethiopia.

in the final analysis. Some observers point to the cageyness and conformity inherent in the practice of reducing the personal biography of a saint to legal formulae and hagiographical archetypes, and to the media exposure this increasingly receives, always with the possibility of controversy. On the one hand, new saints are the product of modern forensic procedures of source criticism and medical scrutiny. On the other, it might be asked whether by relying on science to prove miracles you are missing the point of the miracle, which is to be a sign of something beyond human understanding.

Pope Francis has not let up on the practice of papal canonization. His canonization in October 2015 of Louis and 'Zélie' Martin, rare husband and wife saints (and the parents of nine children, among them St Thérèse of Lisieux) celebrated ordinary lives of labour rewarded with prosperity, adversity met with fortitude, and charity abounding through and beyond family values. It provides a wholesome model for young families to imitate by offering their lives up to God. With these two saints we have come a long way from the desert hermits of Egyptian late antiquity. Or have we? In some places still today, the old forms of sanctity abide (see Figure 12).

Afterword

Prior to theological prescriptions and the papal legislating of sanctity, we should remember that holy fame (*fama sanctitatis*) also belongs to the faithful. It is conjured, encountered, and understood through everyday habits of devotion, and through rumour, gossip, and conversations that elude categorization according to formal distinctions such as imitation and intercession. As well as being a force for social cohesion, the cult of saints can reflect asymmetries and tensions within faith communities. The historian of religion, Robert Orsi, has produced some remarkable ethnographic case studies of twentieth-century Catholic American communities mapping the ambivalent and contested space between heaven and earth, where family and communal relationships were negotiated in the company of saints.

What, he asks, of the prayer for miraculous release from suffering that goes unanswered? Orsi tenderly recounts the life of his Uncle Sal, afflicted with cerebral palsy, and those of countless other 'cripples' and 'shut-ins' (the language of the time) of his Italian-American community. He notes the unwanted role into which their families and neighbours recruited them as the 'specially blessed'. One fear was that their disabilities were a divine punishment inflicted on communities for unspeakable, hidden sin. Much better for people to see them as God's privileged, their bodies, like those of the saints, bearing the ineffable force of his Love. Orsi shows how this habit of co-opting the disabled into positions of pious subjectivity helped resolve the problem of theodicy (God's allowance of suffering in the world), but brought an unnecessary extra burden to their lives through the daily expectations placed upon them to behave with gracious acceptance of their predicament.

His Uncle Sal's anger and resentment found expression and solace in his veneration of St Margaret of Castello (d.1320), a blind and hunchback dwarf of aristocratic birth. Orsi graciously resists the temptation to comprehensively explain his Uncle Sal's devotion to St Margaret. Among its possible meanings, however, he imagines that it affirmed to Sal the worth of such a life, and even perhaps allowed him to subvert and shed the ventriloquized associations the able-bodied inflicted upon him. (I imagine him shouting to the world: 'You can keep your "holy spastics". They do exist, look at St Margaret, but *I'm* not one of them.') Which brings us back to the beginning of this book, and the invention of Superman by a Jewish immigrant. Both experiences entail the imagining of heroic virtue as a means to explore the deeper humanity underlying customary perceptions of difference.

The Church's rules and the practical expertise and creativity of the faithful together align sainthood to 'true north', understood as that cultural reference point that lends particular historical meaning to saints. It has been my aim through the evocation of a series of portraits in landscapes to offer a short introduction to what saints have been and what they might be.

But if 'true north' is historically contingent, then more elusive has been the recovery of sainthood as 'magnetic north', that spark or glimpse the divine presence grants of itself to all saints, and through which their lives are transfigured. Whether through faith or through a humanist's appreciation of the imaginative possibilities of empathy, I hope this book encourages you to explore further the revelation St Augustine experienced in taking up and reading the Bible, the stigmata St Francis and his followers had impressed on their bodies, the spiritual fire that consumed St Symeon Eulabes, or the rapture that, like a powerful eagle, bore Teresa of Ávila up on its wings.

FURTHER READING

CHAPTER 1: INTRODUCTION

H. Brod, *Superman Is Jewish?: How Comic Book Superheroes Came to Serve Truth, Justice, and the Jewish-American Way* (New York, NY: Free Press, 2012).

T. Carlyle, *On Heroes and Hero Worship* (London: James Fraser, 1841).

J. Comaroff and J. Comaroff, *Ethnography and the Historical Imagination* (Boulder, CO: Westview, 1992).

L. S. Cunningham, *A Brief History of Saints* (Oxford: Blackwell, 2004).

D. Farmer, *The Oxford Dictionary of Saints* (5th edn, Oxford: Oxford University Press, 2011).

R. Kieckhefer and G. D. Bond (eds), *Sainthood. Its Manifestations in World Religions* (Berkeley, CA: University of California Press, 1988).

D. MacCulloch, *A History of Christianity: The First Three Thousand Years* (London: Allen Lane, 2009).

S. Tambiah, *The Buddhist Saints of the Forest: A Study in Charisma, Hagiography, Sectarianism and Millennial Buddhism* (Cambridge: Cambridge University Press, 2008).

CHAPTER 2: INVENTING THE SAINTS

L. R. Brody and G. L. Hoffman (eds), *Dura-Europos: Crossroads of Antiquity* (Boston, MA: Yale University Art Gallery, 2011).

P. Brown, *The Cult of Saints. Its Rise and Function in Late Antiquity* (enlarged edn, Chicago, IL: Chicago Press, 2015).

P. Brown, 'The Rise and Function of the Holy Man in Late Antiquity', *Journal of Roman Studies* 61 (1971), 80–101.

D. Caner, *Wandering, Begging Monks: Spiritual Authority and the Promotion of Monasticism in Late Antiquity* (Berkeley, CA: University of California, 2002).

H. Chadwick, *The Penguin History of the Church, vol.1: The Early Church* (London: Penguin, 1993).

K. Cooper, *Band of Angels: The Forgotten World of Early Christian Women* (New York, NY: The Overlook Press, 2013).

Eusebius, *The History of the Church*, trans. G. A. Williamson (London: Penguin Classics, 1965).

C. H. Lawrence, *Medieval Monasticism* (3rd edn, London: Longmans, 2001).

P. Sarris, *Empires of Faith: The Fall of Rome to the Rise of Islam, 500–700* (Oxford: Oxford University Press, 2013).

B. Shaw, *Sacred Violence: African Christians and Sectarian Hatred in the Age of Augustine* (Cambridge: Cambridge University Press, 2011).

CHAPTER 3: SAINTS IN THE MIDDLE AGES

R. Bartlett, *Why Can the Dead Do Such Great Things? Saints and Worshippers from the Martyrs to the Reformation* (Princeton, PA: Princeton University Press, 2013).

L. Brubaker, *Inventing Byzantine Iconoclasm* (London: Bristol Press, 2012).

G. Clark, 'Victricius of Rouen: Praising the Saints', *Journal of Early Christian Studies* 7 (1999), 365–99.

J. Crooks, *The Architectural Setting of the Cult of Saints in the Early Christian West, c.300–c.1200* (Oxford: Oxford University Press, 2000).

M. Dal Santo, *Debating the Saints' Cult in the Age of Gregory the Great* (Oxford: Oxford University Press, 2012).

P. Geary, *Furta Sacra Thefts of Relics in the Central Middle Ages* (rev. edn, Princeton, NJ: Princeton University Press, 1990).

G. Klaniczay, *Holy Rulers and Blessed Princesses Dynastic Cults in Medieval Central Europe* (Cambridge: Cambridge University Press, 2000).

L. Little, *Indispensable Immigrants: The Wine Porters of Northern Italy and their Saint, 1200–1800* (Manchester: Manchester University Press, 2015).

D. MacCulloch, *Silence: A Christian History* (London: Penguin Books, 2013).

R. A. Markus, *The End of Ancient Christianity* (Cambridge: Cambridge University Press, 1990).

O. F. A. Meinardus, *Coptic Saints and Pilgrimages* (Cairo: American University of Cairo Press, 2002).

T. F. X. Noble and T. Head (eds), *Soldiers of Christ Saints and Saints' Lives from Late Antiquity and the Early Middle Ages* (London: Sheed and Ward, 1995).

D. M. Perry, *Sacred Plunder: Venice and the Aftermath of the Fourth Crusade* (Philadelphia, PA: Penn State University Press, 2015).

B. Rosenwein, *To Be a Neighbour of St Peter, The Social Meaning of Cluny's Property* (Ithaca, NY: Cornell University Press, 1989).

R. Van Dam, *Saints and their Miracles in Late Antique Gaul* (Princeton, PA: Princeton University Press, 1993).

A. Vauchez, *Sainthood in the Later Middle Ages*, trans. J. Birrell (Cambridge: Cambridge University Press, 1997).

S. Yarrow, 'Pilgrimage', in *The Routledge History of Medieval Christianity*, ed. R. W. Swanson (London: Routledge, 2015), 159–71.

CHAPTER 4: EARLY MODERN SAINTHOOD

P. Burke, 'How to Become a Counter Reformation Saint', in *Religion and Society in Early Modern Europe,* ed. K. von Greyerz *1500–1800* (London: Routledge, 1984).

E. Cameron, *The European Reformation* (2nd edn, Oxford: Oxford University Press, 2012).

S. Ditchfield, 'Tridentine Worship and the Cult of Saints', in *Cambridge History of Christianity: VI: Reformation and Expansion, 1500–1660*, ed. R. Po-chia Hsia (Cambridge: Cambridge University Press, 2007).

E. Duffy, *The Stripping of the Altars* (2nd edn, New Haven, CT: Yale University Press, 2005).

P. Koudounaris, *Heavenly Bodies: Cult Treasures and Spectacular Saints from the Catacombs* (London: Thames and Hudson, 2013).

D. MacCulloch, *Reformation: Europe's House Divided 1490–1700* (London: Penguin, 2004).

N. Tanner, *Decrees of the Ecumenical Councils*, 2 vols (Georgetown, Washington, DC: Sheed and Ward, 1990).

A. Walsham, *The Reformation of the Landscape Religion, Identity, and Memory in Early Modern Britain and Ireland* (Oxford: Oxford University Press, 2011).

CHAPTER 5: GENDERING THE SAINTS

N. Caciola, *Discerning Spirits: Divine and Demonic Possession in the Middle Ages* (Cornell, NY: Cornell University Press, 2006).

S. L. Deboick, 'Céline Martin's Images of Thérèse and the Creation of a Modern Saint', in *Saints and Sanctity*, eds P. Clarke and T. Claydon, *Studies in Church History* 47 (Woodbridge: Boydell, 2011), 376–89.

O. Hufton, *The Prospect Before Her: A History of Women in Western Europe, 1500–1800* (London: Vintage Books, 1996).

W. Simons, 'In Praise of Faithful Women: Count Robert of Flanders's Defense of Beguines Against the Clementine Decree *Cum de quibusdam mulieribus* (ca.1318–1320)', in *Christianity and Culture in the Middle Age: Essays in honor of J. Van Engen*, eds D. C. Mengel and L. Wolverton (Notre Dame, IN: University of Notre Dame Press, 2015), 331–52.

A.-M. Talbot (ed.), *Holy Women of Byzantium: Ten Saints' Lives in English Translation* (Washington, DC: Dumbarton Oaks, 1996).

D. Weinstein and R. Bell, *Saints and Society: The Two Worlds of Western Christendom, 1000–1700* (Chicago: Chicago University Press, 1983).

CHAPTER 6: THE BLESSED VIRGIN MARY

A. Remensnyder, *La Conquistadora: The Virgin Mary at War and Peace in the Old and New Worlds* (Oxford: Oxford University Press, 2013).

E. M. Rose, *The Murder of William of Norwich: The Origins of the Blood Libel in Medieval Europe* (Oxford: Oxford University Press, 2015).

M. Rubin, *Mother of God: A History of the Virgin Mary* (London: Penguin, 2010).

R. N. Swanson (ed.), *The Church and Mary, Studies in Church History* 39 (Woodbridge: Boydell, 2004).

M. Warner, *Alone of All Her Sex: The Myth and the Cult of the Virgin Mary* (Oxford: Oxford University Press, 2013).

CHAPTER 7: WRITING THE SAINTS

H. Delehaye, *The Legends of the Saints*, trans. T. O'Loughlin (Dublin: Four Courts Press, 1955).

D. C. Douglas, *English Scholars 1660–1730* (London: Eyre & Spottiswoode, 1939).

T. Head, ed., *Medieval Hagiography an Anthology* (London: Routledge, 2001).

T. Heffernan, 'Christian Biography: Foundation to Maturity', in *Historiography in the Middle Ages*, ed. D. M. Deliyannis (Leiden: Brill, 2012).

J. Le Goff, *In Search of Sacred Time: Jacobus de Voragine and the Golden Legend*, trans. L. G. Cochrane (Princeton, NJ: Princeton University Press, 2014).

CHAPTER 8: GLOBALIZING SANCTITY

R. Andrew Chestnut, *Devoted to Death: Santa Muerte, the Skeleton Saint* (Oxford: Oxford University Press, 2012).

W. L. Belcher and M. Kleiner (trans and eds), *The Life and Struggles on Our Mother Walatta Petros written by Galawdewos* (Princeton, NJ: Princeton University Press, 2015).

L. Clossey, *Salvation and Globalisation in the Early Jesuit Missions* (Cambridge: Cambridge University Press, 2008).

A. Greer, *Mohawk Saint: Catherine Tekakwitha and the Jesuits* (Oxford: Oxford University Press, 2005).

A. Greer and J. Bilinkoff (eds), *Colonial Saints Discovering the Holy in the Americas 1500–1800* (London: Routledge, 2003).

A. Hastings (ed.), *A World History of Christianity* (Cambridge: Cambridge University Press, 1999).

W. James, *Vernacular Christianity Essays in the Social Anthropology of Religion* (Oxford: Oxford University Press, 1988).

E. S. Morgan, *Visible Saints: The History of a Puritan Idea* (Ithaca, NY: Cornell University Press, 1963).

R. Rathbone and J. Parker, *African History: A Very Short Introduction* (Oxford: Oxford University Press, 2007).

J. K. Thornton, *The Kongolese Saint Anthony Dona Beatriz Kimpa Vita and the Antonian Movement, 1684–1706* (Cambridge: Cambridge University Press, 1998).

CHAPTER 9: SAINTS IN THE MODERN WORLD

N. Atkin and F. Tallet, *Priests, Prelates and People: A History of European Catholicism Since 1750* (Oxford: Oxford University Press, 2003).

W. Christian, *Person and God in a Spanish Valley* (rev. edn, Princeton, NJ: Princeton University Press, 1989).

R. Clay, 'Saint Geneviève, Iconoclasm and the Transformation of Signs in Revolutionary Paris', in *Striking Images, Iconoclasms Past and Present*, eds S. Boldrick, L. Brubaker, and R. Clay (London: Ashgate, 2013), 97–112.

J. Coleman, 'After Sainthood', in *Saints and Virtues*, ed. J. Stratton Hawley (California, CA: University of California Press, 1987), 205–25.

E. Duffy, *Saints and Sinners: A History of the Popes* (New Haven, CT: Yale University Press, 1997).

M. Heimann, 'Christianity in Western Europe from the Enlightenment', in *A World History of Christianity*, ed. A. Hastings (London, 1999), 459–507.

O. Kharkhordin, *The Collective and the Individual in Russia: A Study of Practices* (Berkeley, CA: University of California Press, 1999).

O. Logan, 'San Luigi Gonzaga: Princeling-Jesuit and Model for Catholic Youth', in *Saints and Sanctity*, eds P. Clarke and T. Claydon, *Studies in Church History* 47 (Woodbridge: Boydell, 2011), 248–57.

R. Orsi, *Between Heaven and Earth: The Religious Worlds People Make and the Scholars Who Study Them* (Princeton, NJ: Princeton University Press, 2005).

J. Shaw, 'The Late Seventeenth and Eighteenth Centuries', in *Christianity: Two Thousand Years*, eds R. Harries and H. Mayr-Harting (Oxford: Oxford University Press, 2001).

M. J. Walsh, 'Pope John Paul II and His Canonizations', *Saints and Sanctity*, eds P. Clarke and T. Claydon, *Studies in Church History* 47 (2011), 415–37.

K. L. Woodward, *Making Saints: How the Catholic Church Determines Who Becomes and Saint, Who Doesn't and Why* (New York, NY: Simon and Schuster, 1990).

PUBLISHER'S ACKNOWLEDGEMENTS

We are grateful for permission to include the following copyright material in this book:

Extracts from pp. 96–7 'here begins the proem to the miracles of St Thelthryth the virgin' from *Goscelin of Saint-Bertin: The Hagiography of the Female Saints of Ely*, edited by Rosalind C. Love (Oxford University Press 2004). By permission of Oxford University Press.

The publisher and author have made every effort to trace and contact all copyright holders before publication. If notified, the publisher will be pleased to rectify any errors or omissions at the earliest opportunity.

INDEX

Index